IT'S
NEGOTIABLE

THE HOW-TO HANDBOOK
OF WIN/WIN TACTICS

Peter B. Stark

Pfeiffer
& COMPANY

Amsterdam • Johannesburg • Oxford
San Diego • Sydney • Toronto

This publication is designed to provide accurate and authori-tative information in regard to the subject matter covered. It is sold with the understanding that the publisher is not engaged in rendering legal, accounting, or other professional service. If legal advice or other expert assistance is required, the services of a competent professional person should be sought. *From a Declaration of Principles jointly adopted by a Committee of the American Bar Association and a Committee of Publishers.*

Page Compositor: Lee Ann Hubbard
Cover: Tom Lewis, Inc.
Production Editor: Katharine Pechtimaldjian
Editorial Assistant: Susan Rachmeler

ISBN: 0-89384-254-0 (trade paper)
      0-88390-418-7 (hardcover)

Printed in the United States of America.

Printing 1 2 3 4 5 6 7 8 9 10

DEDICATION

This book is dedicated to my wife and children...
three of the greatest negotiators whose love and inspiration
influence my life on a daily basis.

CONTENTS

INTRODUCTION:
WHY ANOTHER BOOK
ON NEGOTIATION?

The purpose of this book is to provide you, the reader, with the skills and tools necessary to be a great negotiator. The philosophy behind the approach used in this book is that as a negotiator, you have an obligation to help your counterpart in negotiations achieve a win/win outcome. Why? Because few negotiations are one-time affairs. I used to feel differently about this. Several years ago I bought a new motorhome from a dealership and was proud of the major price reduction I had negotiated. I drove the motorhome away saying to my wife, "I think that might be the best deal I've ever negotiated." One month later I drove the motorhome back to the dealership to have warranty-covered work done. The dealership had gone out of business. The next closest dealership that would honor the warranty was 120 miles from my home. What goes around comes around—I lost!

Some people have asked, "If you're so big on a win/win outcome, why do you place such a great emphasis on strategies and tactics?" My answer is twofold. First, not everyone you negotiate with has a desire to create a win/win outcome. I have negotiated with many counterparts who could care less if I blatantly lost. Second, to create a win/win outcome, you need to have an effective strategy. In most situations, strategies and tactics are critical to one's success.

Note that I have chosen to use the word *counterpart* rather than *opponent*. How you view those you negotiate with will have a lot to do with your ability to negotiate a win/win outcome.

Although great negotiators drive a hard bargain, most have the reputation of being both fair and trustworthy. When you have these qualities, people will come back and renegotiate with you at a later date. This book will give you the skills and tools to be a win/win negotiator.

1

WHAT IS NEGOTIATION?

What do you think of when you hear the word *negotiation*? The president trying to persuade Congress to pass his budget? The former Los Angeles chief of police, Daryl Gates, trying to persuade the L.A. City Council he was worthy of retaining his job? Exxon fighting with the environmentalists to decide how much the company should pay to clean up the Alaskan shoreline marred by the *Valdez* oil spill? A department manager trying to secure more personnel or a larger budget? Labor and management locked in a twelfth-hour contract struggle? Buyer and seller haggling over the price of a house or a car? Most of us do tend to think of negotiation in terms of such win/lose scenarios.

Recently, at a San Diego State University-sponsored seminar on negotiation, the following question was posed to participants: How often do you negotiate—often, seldom, or never?

Surprisingly, over 36 percent of the respondents answered *seldom* or *never*. However, this was a trick question! The correct answer is *always*. Everything in life is negotiated, under all conditions, at all times: from asking your significant other to take out the morning garbage to merging into a freeway lane in rush-hour traffic, from determining what time to schedule an appointment with a client to deciding which 11:00 news program to watch with your family—every aspect of your life is spent in some form of negotiation.

Gerard I. Nierenberg, the author of the first book on the formalized process of negotiation, *The Art of Negotiating*, and president of the New York City-based Negotiation Institute Inc., states that "whenever people exchange ideas with the intention of changing relationships, whenever they confer for agreement, then they are negotiating."[1] The late Israel Unterman, a professor of management at San Diego State University, expands Nierenberg's definition slightly to note that "negotiation is conducted neither to widen nor to breach the relationship, but to form a new or different configuration."[2]

In short, most of us are constantly involved in negotiations to one degree or another for a good part of any given day. Negotiation should be considered as a positive way of structuring the communication process.

Typical Negotiated Transactions

Here is a list of some typical transactions in which you can improve your position by negotiating.

1. Price, terms, and accessory items on an automobile purchase
2. Price, terms, and length of escrow on a home purchase
3. Price and terms on an appliance purchase
4. Turnaround time for when a mechanic repairs and returns your car
5. Which evening television program your family will watch
6. What clothes your children will wear

7. Your salary
8. Work projects
9. Hourly rate a new client is willing to pay
10. A date for an event

Negotiation Situations

In what other areas in your daily routine could you improve your position by negotiating? List them here:

1. _____

   _____

2. _____

   _____

3. _____

   _____

4. _____

   _____

5. _____

   _____

6. _____

   _____

7. _____

   _____

8. _____

   _____

How Good a Negotiator Are You?

Like any management skill, negotiation can be learned, practiced, and mastered. Here is a questionnaire on the personal characteristics necessary to be a great negotiator. It will help you determine where you have strengths as a negotiator and where you may need improvement. Circle the number that best reflects where you fall on the scale. The higher the number, the more the characteristic describes you. When you have finished, add up your numbers and put the total in the space provided.

1. I enjoy dealing with other people, and I am committed to creating a win/win outcome.

   1 2 3 4 5 6 7 8 9 10

2. I enjoy solving problems and coming up with creative solutions.

   1 2 3 4 5 6 7 8 9 10

3. I am willing to ask as many questions as it takes to get the needed information to make the best decision.

   1 2 3 4 5 6 7 8 9 10

4. I do not take my counterpart's strategies, tactics, and comments personally.

   1 2 3 4 5 6 7 8 9 10

5. I like to uncover the needs, wants, and motivations of my counterpart so I can help her/him achieve her/his goals.

   1 2 3 4 5 6 7 8 9 10

6. I am able to think clearly under pressure.

   1   2   3   4   5   6   7   8   9   10

7. I have good self-esteem and tend to have a high level of aspiration and expectation.

   1   2   3   4   5   6   7   8   9   10

8. I recognize the power of strategies and tactics and use them frequently.

   1   2   3   4   5   6   7   8   9   10

9. I am willing to compromise to solve problems when necessary.

   1   2   3   4   5   6   7   8   9   10

10. I am a good listener.

   1   2   3   4   5   6   7   8   9   10

Grand Total: _____

Scoring

90+: You have the characteristics of a great negotiator. You recognize what negotiation requires, and you are willing to apply yourself accordingly.

80-89: You should do well as a negotiator, but you have some areas that need improvement.

70-79: You have an understanding of negotiation but can improve in some important areas.

0-70: Go over the questions again. You may have been hard on yourself, or you may have identified some key areas that you will need to concentrate on when you negotiate. Repeat this evaluation again when you have finished reading this book and applied the principles it outlines.

2

NEGOTIATION'S FIVE POSSIBLE OUTCOMES

A negotiation will end in one of five possible outcomes: lose/lose, lose/win, win/lose, win/win, or nothing happens (no negative or positive consequences). In most situations, you should strive for a win/win outcome.

Lose/Lose

Lose/lose is the outcome when neither party achieves his or her needs or wants and is reluctant to negotiate with the same counterpart again. In 1987 I tried to negotiate a $30,000 printing contract with a major corporation in San Diego. I thought I had the contract, but at the last minute the client informed me the company had chosen another printer that had given a lower bid. At that precise moment, the client had won, I had lost. The client had found a better price and felt the competitor would give the quality and service to back up the price. One month later, I received a call from the client informing me that the printer had done an awful job on their brochure. To top it off, the competitor's service had been poor and the client no longer trusted the company. Because the printer's delays caused the company to miss having its new product brochure ready in time for the only industry trade show of year, the client lost also.

Lose/Win and Win/Lose

The second and third possible outcomes of negotiation are the win/lose and the lose/win. The difference between the two is which side of the fence you end up on. In some negotiations, you will be the winner and your counterpart will be the loser. In other negotiations, the roles will be reversed. If you have ever lost a negotiation, you know that the feeling is not pleasant. The significant problem in a win/lose or lose/win outcome is that one party walks away without meeting his or her needs or wants. And more important, the loser is likely to refuse to renegotiate with the winner. Ultimately, this sets up the potential for a future lose/lose outcome.

In my early sales career, I had a client who used to purchase printing on a regular basis. This person had a reputation for being both a shark and a jerk. Not only would he beat down my price, he would then be rude and verbally abusive through every step of the job. After several jobs, it was apparent the stress of working with this individual was costing me more time, energy, and grief than the jobs were worth. With time, I learned that quoting his jobs at twice our normal markup, and not budging on the price, eliminated this lopsided relationship.

Remember, when you create a win/lose or lose/win situation, the loser will most likely refuse to negotiate with the same counterpart again. In 1988, during a six-week course in negotiation at San Diego State University, one of my students continually created win/lose outcomes, with himself in the winner's circle. By the sixth week, there was not one person in the class who would negotiate with him. Creating win/lose or lose/win is not good business!

Win/Win

In almost all negotiations, you should strive for a win/win outcome, in which the needs and goals of both parties have been met. Both parties will walk away with a positive feeling and will be willing to negotiate with each other again. In the negotiation workshops I present, it is rewarding to see the excitement in participants' faces when they both realize they have created a win/win outcome.

Four Keys to Creating a Win/Win Outcome

There are four keys to creating a win/win outcome.

First, do not narrow your negotiation down to one issue. If you do focus on just one issue, you create a situation where you will have a winner and a loser. The most common example of narrowing a negotiation to one issue is arguing over the price of something. Many other factors besides price can be brought into the negotiation, such as delivery fees, timing, quality, other goods and services, and so on.

Second, realize that your counterpart does not have the same needs and wants you do. If you do not take this factor into consideration, you negotiate from the framework that your loss is your counterpart's gain. With that attitude, it is virtually impossible to create a win/win outcome.

Third, do not assume you know your counterpart's needs. It's very common for negotiators to assume that they know exactly what their counterpart wants. For example, a salesperson knows that the buyer wants to buy the product or service at the lowest possible price. Although this may be true, the buyer may have a much more powerful need that influences his or her decision to buy the product or service. By asking good questions you may find, for example, that a buyer's biggest concern is that his boss perceives his purchase decision as a good one.

A great example of erroneously assuming one's counterpart's needs happened in the acrimonious battles between the Los Angeles City Council and Daryl Gates, former chief of police. At the conclusion of the first Rodney King trial, Los Angeles experienced the worst rioting in the history of the city. The rampage left 57 dead and 2,383 injured. Burning and looting destroyed thousands of businesses, causing more than $785 million in damage.[3] Much of the blame for the extensiveness of the riots fell on the ill-preparedness of the Los Angeles Police Department. Mayor Tom Bradley publicly asked for Gates's resignation, as did the city council and two citizen commissions. The assumption was that Gates, like most public officials, would want to avoid negative publicity and thus would cooperate.

Yet the more negative publicity Gates received, the more he dug in his heels and refused to leave office. He said he would not resign unless his eligibility date for retirement was moved up. The city council obliged. He then publicly set a June 30 retirement date. Gates next hinted that he would not resign until several of his top-ranking captains were promoted. The council did not agree to this point, and Gates soon amended his retirement date to mid-July, possibly leaving the city with two police chiefs.

You might be asking yourself why the city council didn't fire Gates. Because of a technicality in the city charter, neither the city council nor the mayor had the power to fire the chief of police. A more important reason the city council didn't press for Gates's retirement was fear. It had been well documented that the Los Angeles Police Department had secret files on each elected public official, and the council members feared what those files might contain.

It appeared from all sides that the mayor and council were on a string under the chief's control until the council changed its tactic and started to focus on taking away or reducing the chief's $124,000-a-year pension. From the day the council started discussing the possibility of reducing the chief's pension, the leverage and outcomes in the negotiation began to change. On Monday, June 15, a buoyant Gates said his threat to remain in office had been a "bluff" to gain attention for his dispute with "crummy little politicians" over a promotional list for captains.

In this case, the erroneous assumption was that Gates would be motivated by a need to avoid negative publicity, when in fact his more important needs lay elsewhere.

Fourth, you need to believe point number two in your heart. Most novice negotiators acknowledge that their counterpart most likely does not have the same needs and wants as they do, but when they get into an actual negotiation, this acknowledgment vanishes from their mind.

A famous incident with Chrysler Corporation provides a great example of creating a win/win outcome. In the late 1970s, when Chrysler was fighting for its financial survival, its only hope was obtaining a guaranteed subsidized loan from the United States government. At the time, the majority of Americans were dead set against the government bailing out any aspect of private industry. Chrysler's chairman, Lee Iacocca, went before Congress and told the politicians he was representing not only himself and Chrysler's 147,000 employees but also Chrysler's 4,700 dealers and their 150,000 employees, plus Chrysler's 19,000 suppliers and their 250,000 employees. Then Iacocca divided up Congress district by district and informed each representative and senator exactly how many people would be adversely affected in his or her district if the loan was not granted. With superior planning and research, Iacocca was able to transform the needs and goals of the politicians into his needs and goals. When the vote was taken, it passed by a margin of 2 to 1 in the House and by a vote of 53 to 44 in the Senate. With this approval, Chrysler borrowed $1.2 billion for ten years.

On April 15, 1983, just three years after the loan's origination date, Iacocca presented the United States government with a check for $813,487,500. This check paid Chrysler's obligation in full. Thus, everyone won—Chrysler, Chrysler's suppliers, the U.S. government, and all the banks that contributed to the loan. Even the politicians who voted for the loan package felt they benefited by being associated with Chrysler's success.

No Outcome

The fifth possible outcome is no outcome: neither party wins or loses. For example, a person who owned a large commercial piece of real estate decided to sell his property. The reason for selling was that the city government was considering rezoning the area where the property was located. The property owner felt the rezoning was going to lower the property value. A real estate agent was called to list the property. In the meeting, the real estate agent, who was a member of the zoning commission, told the property owner that they had received erroneous information and no rezoning would take place. The agent recommended that the owner hold on to the property, rather than sell. The property owner accepted the agent's advice. In this particular negotiation, nothing happened.

In most negotiations, it will be in your best interest to have a cooperative attitude to help develop a win/win atmosphere. When each party obtains something of greater value for something on which he or she places a lower value, both win. You may have each wished for more, but at least you are both satisfied.

3

THE THREE CRITICAL ELEMENTS: TIME, INFORMATION, AND POWER

The three most critical elements in negotiation are time (the period over which the negotiation process takes place), information (the more you have, the better), and power (which comes in many forms).

Time

Most people think of negotiation as an event that has a definite beginning and ending. Furthermore, most people consider the negotiation to start and end with the actual interactive process between the two parties. Nothing could be further from the truth.

An acquaintance sought advice on what strategy to use to ask for a raise during her annual review with her boss. All the options she had considered dealt with the actual review session. What she had not considered was all the preplanning and information gathering needed to create a powerful negotiation. She had not taken into account such things as documenting her accomplishments over the previous year; finding out what her boss's needs and goals are and how she can help him achieve his goals; finding out what types of raises her boss has given in the past and in what amounts; and having a clear vision on what goals she wants to achieve in the negotiation. In this example, the negotiation began the day our seminar participant started working for the company and will continue to her next employment opportunity. Most negotiations, like life, are a continuous process.

Time plays a critical role in negotiations. Most often, negotiations will conclude in the final 20 percent of the time allowed. This aspect of negotiation follows an interesting rule that seems to apply to life in general. It's called the 80/20 rule, or Pareto's law (after Vilfredo Pareto, the Italian economist and sociologist who defined it). It states: "Twenty percent of what you do produces 80 percent of the results; conversely, 80 percent of what you do produces only 20 percent of the results."

In negotiation, this means that 80 percent of your results are generally agreed upon in the last 20 percent of your time. We consistently see this phenomenon in the seminars we present. As the participants negotiate with each other, the seminar leader periodically tells them how much time they have left. Normally, the majority of the negotiations are concluded in the final two minutes.

Time and deadlines can favor either side, depending on the circumstances. Here are a few suggestions that will help you bring time to your side of the negotiations.

1. *Have patience.* Because most concessions and set-tlements will occur in the last 20 percent of the available time, remain levelheaded and wait for the right moment to act. As a general rule, patience pays.
2. *If there are benefits to resolving the negotiation quickly, sell your counterpart on the value added to him or her.* There will be times when one or both parties will benefit if negotiations are resolved quickly.

3. *Realize deadlines can be moved, changed, or eliminated.* As your deadline comes near, do not panic. Change your deadline. Have you ever wondered how many of the people running to the post office at the last minute on April 15 have refunds coming to them? Even without a refund, people still have the opportunity to file an extension, giving them another four months to send in their forms.

4. *In most negotiations you are better off if you know your counterpart's deadline and he or she does not know yours.* As you near the point that you perceive as the other's deadline, his or her stress level will increase and he or she will most likely make concessions.

5. *Remember that generally you will not achieve the best outcome quickly.* Although there are exceptions to this rule, generally you are better off changing your deadline and moving on in the negotiation, slowly and with perseverance.

Information

Most often, the side with the most information will receive the better outcome in a negotiation. Why, then, do people fail to get adequate information prior to a negotiation? Because, as we mentioned earlier, they tend to perceive the negotiation as the actual interaction between two parties. People seldom think about the information they need until this fact hits them in the actual negotiation.

A negotiation is not an event, it is a *process*. It starts long before the face-to-face encounter. One reason you have to start preparing much earlier is that during the actual negotiation, it is likely that your counterpart will conceal his or her true interests, needs, and motivations. Your chances of getting this information during the actual negotiation is relatively remote.

The earlier you start, the easier it is to obtain information. People are more willing to give out information prior to starting any formal interaction. Before buying my wife's car, I went to several dealerships asking questions about the models we were interested in, the financing plans available, and how willing they were to deal.

Where do you get information? From anyone who has knowledge that will help you in your negotiation. You can find useful material by researching facts and statistics, talking to someone who has negotiated with your counterpart in the past, talking to your counterpart, or speaking with friends, relatives, and others who've been in similar negotiations.

Advanced Preparation in Negotiation

In negotiations, advanced preparation is critical. The more information you have, the better off you will be. Also, it will be in your best interest to have a clear set of goals going into the negotiation. You should set your goals based on the information you collect. The following questionnaire will help you collect the information you will need.

Points of View Questionnaire

Your Side	Counterpart's Side
Topic:	Topic:
Available Facts:	Available Facts:
Negotiable Issues:	Negotiable Issues:
Needs of Negotiators:	Needs of Negotiators:
Position on Issues:	Known Position on Issues:
Strategy and Tactics:	Strategy and Tactics:

Power

The word *power* has had a bad connotation for many years. It has received this reputation because most people associate the word with one side dominating or overpowering the other. I define *power* as the ability to influence people or situations. With this definition, power is neither good nor bad. It is the abuse of power that is bad.

Types of Power

There are ten types of power that *can* influence the outcome of a negotiation. I emphasize the word *can*, because if one has power but doesn't use it, the power adds no value to the negotiation.

1. *Position.* Some measure of power is conferred based on one's formal position in an organization. A marketing manager can influence the decisions that affect the marketing department. However, the marketing manager has little authority or power in influencing the decisions that affect the finance department.

2. *Legitimacy.* Certain positions of authority confer legitimate power. The pope of the Catholic Church holds this type of power. Catholics look to the pope for guidance in areas such as marriage, divorce, or abortion.

3. *Knowledge or expertise.* People who have knowledge or expertise can wield tremendous power. Of course, knowledge in itself is not powerful. It is the use and application of knowledge and expertise that confers power. Thus, you could be an incredibly bright person and still be powerless.

4. *Character*. The more trustworthy individuals are, the more power they will have in negotiations. The big issue here is whether they do what they say they are going to do.

5. *Rewards*. Those who are able to bestow rewards or perceived rewards hold power. Supervisors, with their ability to give raises, hold power over employees.

6. *Punishment*. Those who have the ability to create a negative outcome for their counterpart have the power of punishment. Managers hold this type of power with their ability to reprimand and fire employees. State troopers and highway patrol officers also have this power with their ability to give out speeding tickets.

7. *Sex*. Dealing with someone of the opposite sex can confer power. I have videotaped many negotiation case studies in which the turning point was when a woman casually touched a man's hand or arm to make her point.

8. *Behavior style*. You are most likely one or a combination of the following behavioral styles: (a) analytical, process oriented, methodical; (b) driven, task oriented, goal directed, bottom-line focused; (c) supportive, relationship oriented, focused on feelings; (d) some blend of the other three. Which behavioral style is the most appropriate depends on the situation. Someone going through a divorce who wants to maintain a good relationship with his or her spouse and children would want to use the supportive style. The real power behind knowledge of behavior styles lies in your ability to adapt your style to the situation.

9. *No power.* In some instances giving up all power can be very powerful. If a kidnapper threatens a hostage with death enough times, the hostage may just challenge the kidnapper to go ahead and kill him. At the point that the hostage no longer fears death, the kidnapper loses his power.

10. *Crazy.* This may sound funny, but bizarre or irrational behavior can confer a tremendous amount of power. Every organization has someone who blows up or behaves in an irrational way when confronted with problems. Those who have been exposed to this type of behavior tend to avoid such individuals. Some people in organizations are not given many tasks to accomplish because others are afraid to ask them.

Most people have more power than they think. I believe there is a link between one's self-esteem and the amount of power one believes one has. It has been demonstrated that people with high self-esteem feel they have more viable options in negotiations. People with low self-esteem do not perceive themselves as having viable alternatives. These are the same for people who feel they lack the power to act. Powerless people become apathetic, which means they do not stand a fair chance when they enter a negotiation.

Rules About Power

When entering into a negotiation, there are some rules to remember about power.

1. *Seldom does one side have all the power.* Even when you go to banks asking for a business loan, you, the entrepreneur or customer, still have power: the power to decide which bank you will apply to;

the power to decide what interest rate you will pay; and the power to decide whether you will put up your home as collateral.

2. *Power may be real or apparent.* When I was a proctor in the sociology department at San Diego State University, I knew that cheating was a problem, but I had never made a focused effort to stop the offenders. I figured I would use multiple tests on the final to prevent cheating. Unfortunately, when the term was ending I didn't have time to scramble the finals, so I had to resort to Plan B. As I was passing out the tests, I announced that I would uphold the university's "policy" on cheating. As I completed handing out the test, one bold student asked what the policy was. My response was simple: "If you need to ask, then you don't want to know." This was the first time I had ever seen all sixty students staring at their own paper. Does the university have a policy on cheating? I don't know. But in this situation, whether the power was real or apparent didn't matter. The students *perceived* that I had the power.

3. *Power exists only to the point at which it is accepted.* When returning from a trip to Europe, I noted at the airport that all the ticketing agents for the economy class had at least a twenty-minute line to check baggage. Yet the business and first class agents had not one person in line. Not wanting to wait in line, I boldly took my baggage and tickets up to the business class agent and got my seat assignment. (I would have gone up to the first class counter, but I didn't want to push my luck.)

4. *Power relationships can change over time.* This is one of the hardest lessons I have ever learned. In my youth, I had the same girlfriend from the seventh to the eleventh grades. At the time, I was proud to say I had the power in this relationship. I chose which activities we would become involved in, what friends we would have, and where we would go on our dates. Giving her flowers was not in my repertoire. After all, I didn't need them. And then something happened that sent me into a tailspin. Marilyn, my girlfriend, was asked out by the student body president. As if that weren't enough, Brutus was also the starting quarterback for the football team. Overnight, I was sending cards and roses and begging for a date. It was my first real-life lesson that win/lose negotiations eventually end in lose/lose.

In relationships, the side with the least commitment generally holds the most power. If one party is highly committed to the relationship and the other is not, the former will generally have less power in the relationship.

5. *Test your power.* You will never know how much power you have until you test reality. The chances are, you have more power than you think. Once again, power is neither good nor bad. The abuse of power is what is bad.

4

QUESTIONING SKILLS: HOW TO UNCOVER YOUR OPPONENT'S NEEDS

To create a win/win outcome, you need to know your counterpart's needs, wants, and goals. You need to be like a detective, searching for any information that will help you to better understand the motivations and true intentions of your adversary. While you are using the questioning process, pay close attention to your counterpart's words and actions, reactions, mannerisms, and gestures, as they will offer clues to his or her real thoughts.

Skillful questioning will gain you the maximum amount of information possible for developing your negotiation strategy. Unfortunately, questioning skills are very seldom taught, with the possible exception of law courses. Remember, the side with the most information usually wins the negotiation.

Asking good questions in negotiations involves three decisions: what questions to ask, how to word them, and when to ask them. I'm reminded of an inexperienced lawyer who was defending a man accused of biting off another man's ear in a brawl. The lawyer asked one of the prosecution's witnesses whether he had actually seen the defendant bite off the man's ear. The witness replied, "No." The lawyer should have quit right there and rested his case. Instead, he went on to ask the witness how he absolutely knew that it was the defendant who had been in the brawl. The witness replied, "Because I saw your client spit out that man's ear." This was the wrong question at the wrong time.

The guidelines in this chapter will help you in formulating your questions.

Why People Ask Questions

People ask questions for ten main reasons. To

1. Gain information
2. Check understanding and level of interest
3. Determine your counterpart's behavioral style
4. Gain participation
5. Give information
6. Start someone thinking
7. Bring back attention to the subject
8. Reach agreement
9. Reduce tension
10. Give positive strokes

Gain Information

Obtaining information is the most obvious reason for asking questions. You try to fill in gaps where you lack information. This point is mentioned first to emphasize that when you do not have all the answers, or when you are not sure whether you have the right answers, ask. Don't assume anything when you are negotiating.

Check Understanding and Level of Interest

How much is your counterpart interested in the outcome of the negotiation? Is he or she committed? You may want to send up a trial balloon by asking whether, for example, your counterpart would be willing to take a specified amount less than his or her asking price. Or, you could ask a question to uncover how technically sound your counterpart is on the topic you are negotiating.

Determine Your Counterpart's Behavioral Style

What type of person is your counterpart? Where is he or she coming from? Is he or she an experienced negotiator? an honest person? a decisive person? Questions that reveal this kind of information will influence how you negotiate. Different people require different strategies.

Gain Participation

Any time you can ask your counterpart a question and let him or her talk, you will gain a twofold benefit. First, your counterpart will like you better. Second, you will learn more about your counterpart than he or she will learn about you. Another important aspect to this point is that you should get your counterpart to talk whenever you've said something that he or she didn't agree with or understand. Getting your counterpart to talk will have a calming effect. Also, you will be supplied with more information to help your counterpart meet his or her needs.

Give Information

Many times, you will want to give your counterpart information so that he or she will better understand your needs and goals. Example: "Did you know that the Kelly Bluebook value of your car is only $2,100?" This type of question can also be used as a test to see whether your counterpart recognizes if your information is correct.

Start Someone Thinking

Questions that ask for someone's opinion are a great source of information. Asking for people's opinions also tells them you are interested in them and what they have to say. Examples: "Can you tell me why you like living in this neighborhood? What is your feeling about some of the problems in the neighborhood and how they can be solved?" Once again, the more you can get your counterpart to talk, the more information you will have for basing your strategy.

Bring Back Attention to the Subject

Some people have a habit of beating around the bush. Maybe they are intentionally avoiding a sensitive topic. Appropriate questions can help keep the conversation moving along and heading toward your goal.

Salespeople are often taught to find out something personal about a prospect and use this information as a starting point for their presentation. Talking about the personal side is fine, but eventually you will need to change your questioning pattern and get answers for the real reasons you are meeting. This requires asking questions that will focus attention back on your desired subject. For example: "Can we get back to the salary issue and benefits package once again? Is it possible to increase the starting salary by $5,000 so I can maintain parity with my current benefits package?"

Reach Agreement

Questions to reach agreement can serve as a trial balloon. They test your proposal to see whether your counterpart is in agreement. Suppose a seller is asking $150,000 for his house. Because it needs landscaping and a new roof, you ask whether he is willing to take $140,000. The value of this type of question is that the answer lets you know how far apart your goals are from your counterpart's.

Reduce Tension

At times negotiations can become tense. When things go wrong, it is helpful to ask questions that will gain further information about your counterpart's viewpoint. With this added information, you may be able to restructure the negotiation. Example: "Every time we talk about mandatory drug testing for all employees, you seem to be adamantly opposed. Can you share a little about why you are opposed to mandatory drug testing?"

Another type of question that reduces tension is one that introduces humor into the situation. Recently, a friend was trying to negotiate an extra two days of paid vacation a year. When her boss gave her a blunt no, the room became thick with tension. Her timely response, "Does this mean a raise is also out of the question?"

Give Positive Strokes

Simply put, a positive strokes question says, "I want to make you feel important." Sometimes you even know the answer and still ask the question. The expression of caring that you give your counterpart is what is important. Suppose your counterpart has received three phone calls from complaining customers and had two employee interruptions during your fifteen-minute meeting. You might ask, "Are you having a tough day?

Two Main Types of Questions

Questions may be closed-ended and restrictive, or they may be open-ended and expansive.

Restrictive or Closed Questions

Restrictive or closed questions usually seek a specific bit of information, and the answer is often a simple yes or no. This type of question is also useful for directing a conversation to a desired area and for gaining commitment to a definite position.

Here are some typical examples of restrictive questions: "Do you think your price is fair?" "Do you want to work on Saturday or Sunday?" "You will send the revised quotation to me by Monday, right?"

Ask restrictive questions when all you want is a yes or no answer or to break the ice when you sense that your counterpart is uncomfortable negotiating with you.

The object of restrictive questioning isn't so much to get information as it is to start the conversation or create a more agreeable atmosphere.

Expansive or Open Questions

Generally speaking, open-ended questions will yield much more useful information than closed-ended questions will. Open-ended questions tend to be more informative because they do not lead your counterpart in any specific direction. They are also more productive in uncovering your counterpart's objectives, needs, wants, and current situation. Finally, an open-ended question is much more effective in revealing your counterpart's behavioral style. Simple yes or no answers will not reveal their point of reference. Open questions tend to provide a window into your counterpart's mind.

Here are some typical open-ended questions: "How do you feel about moving out of your home before Christmas?" "You seem to be upset with my offer. Which aspects of the offer seem to be the biggest problems?"

When my company first started, Sharon, our vice president of accounting, used to ask me to make the company's bank deposit while on my sales calls. Because many of my accounts were downtown, she felt it was convenient for me to stop at the bank, which was also located downtown. To find out whether I was available, Sharon would always ask, "Are you going downtown today?" A simple yes or no question. Because I hated taking the deposit into the bank each day, I lied to her. Finally Sharon caught on to my deception and changed her style of question. Now she asks, "Peter, which clients are you going to see today?" When I tell her who is on my schedule, she replies, "Great. As long as you are downtown seeing clients, will you make the bank deposit?" That type of questioning yields much more information and makes it much more difficult to give the answer no.

Although there are many different types of questions, most will fall into the open or closed category.

Keys to Proper Questioning

The manner in which you ask a question is as important as the content of the question. Since you want to gain the maximum information about your opponent's needs and motivations, you will want to structure your questions carefully. Following are several key points that will help you gain accurate information.

1. *Have a questioning plan.* When you are negotiating, it is important to have a goal in mind and to have

a questioning plan that will help you achieve that goal. What type of information will help you in making a good decision? How will you go about getting that information? Will you be direct? Will you disguise your questions? A questioning plan will put you in the action mode, and it will put your counterpart in a reaction mode responding to your question. With your counterpart reacting, you are in the driver's seat.

2. *Know your counterpart.* The more you can find out about your counterpart, the better you can target your questions. Based on greater knowledge, your questions can be better directed and more specific.

3. *Move from the broad to the narrow.* In the question sequence, it is helpful to start with broad questions. Then, as you gain answers to broad questions, you can refine and hone your questions to eventually yield specific information. Example: "Did you keep the maintenance records on your car?" "Yes." "What type of maintenance records did you keep?" "Changing the oil and replacing tires." "How often did you change your oil?" "Every 3,000 miles." "What kind of oil did you use?" and so on.

4. *Have proper timing.* We've all experienced situations where we asked the wrong question at the wrong time. It is important that you be sensitive to your counterpart's needs and feelings. If your counterpart is not receptive to your question, or finds it offensive, two things happen. First, you will not gain the amount of information you could have if your question had been properly timed. Second, with offensive questioning, your counter-

part may not want to negotiate with you again. Asking your significant other how his or her diet is going while he or she is eating a big dessert is a good example of bad timing.

5. *Build on previous responses.* This point is similar to point number 3. As you gain more information, your questions can be more specific. Negotiators who use this technique tend to be better listeners. They are always listening for information that they can dive into for more clarification. The more information they have, the better decisions they make. Peter Falk's Lt. Columbo is a master of this technique: "Just one more question: If you weren't at the murder scene, how did you know the weapon was a knife?"

6. *Ask permission to ask a question.* Asking permission is the polite thing to do. It is also effective because most people will not say no if you ask their permission to ask them a question. Finally, asking permission starts the swing toward agreement. Once your counterpart has granted you permission, he or she is more likely to give you a complete answer. Columbo is also master of this technique. He is forever going back to the suspect and asking, "Can I ask you just one more question?"

A successful negotiator has to know the wants, needs, and motivations of his counterpart. The easiest and quickest way to uncover them is through successful and skillful questioning. With practice, you will find yourself asking better questions, and the information gained will be increasingly valuable.

5

LISTENING SKILLS: A POWERFUL KEY TO SUCCESSFUL NEGOTIATING

Unfortunately, few negotiators know how to be good listeners. And negotiators who are poor listeners miss numerous opportunities in their counterpart's words. Statistics indicate that the normal, untrained listener is likely to understand and retain only about 50 percent of a conversation. This relatively poor percentage drops to an even less impressive 25 percent retention rate forty-eight hours later. This means that recall of particular conversations will usually be inaccurate and incomplete.

Many communication problems in negotiations are attributable to poor listening skills. To be a good listener, you must attempt to be objective. This means you must try to understand the intentions behind your counterpart's communication—and not just what you want to understand. With everything your counterpart tells you, you must ask yourself: "Why did he tell me that? What does he think my reaction should be? Was he being honest?" and so on.

The best negotiators almost always turn out to be the best listeners as well. Why does the correlation exist? Invariably, the best negotiators have been observing the communication skills, both verbal and nonverbal, of their counterparts. They have heard and noted how other negotiators effectively use word choice and sentence structure.

They have also practiced listening for the vocal skills, such as the rate of speech, pitch, and tonal quality.

Experts on listening suggest that we all make at least one major listening mistake each day, and for negotiators, such mistakes can be costly. It seems obvious, but studies prove that the most successful salespeople are those who are able to uncover more needs than their less successful colleagues. This finding is significant, since salespeople make their living by negotiating.

Three Pitfalls of Listening

Negotiators tend to run into three pitfalls that hinder effective listening. First, many think that negotiating is primarily a job of persuasion, and to them persuasion means talking. These people see talking as an active role and listening as a passive role. They tend to forget that it is difficult to persuade other people when you don't know what motivates these people.

Second, people tend to overprepare for what they are going to say and to use their listening time waiting for their next turn to speak. While anticipating their next chance, they may miss vital information they could use later in the negotiation.

Third, we all have emotional filters or blinders that prevent us from hearing what we do not want to hear. In my early sales career, I seemed to always waste time with clients who I thought would buy printing from me but never did. Now I very seldom have that problem. What experience has shown me is that the people who used to waste my time had no intention of using my services. If I had been a better listener, I would have been able to pick up on their true feelings.

Attentive Listening Skills

Great listening does not come easily. It is hard work. There are two major types of listening skills, attentive and interactive. The following attentive skills will help you better receive the true meanings your counterparts are trying to convey.

1. *Be motivated to listen.* When you know that the person with the most information usually receives the better outcome in a negotiation, you have an incentive to be a better listener. It is wise to set goals for all the different kinds of information you would like to receive from your counterpart. The more you can learn, the better off you will be. The real challenge comes when you need to motivate yourself to listen to someone you do not like.

2. *If you must speak, ask questions.* The goal is to get more specific and better refined information. To do so, you will have to continue questioning your counterpart. Your questioning sequence will be moving from the broad to the narrow, and eventually you will have the information to make the best decision. The second reason to continue asking questions is that it will help you uncover your counterpart's needs and wants.

3. *Be alert to nonverbal cues.* Although it is critical to listen to what is being said, it is equally important to understand the attitudes and motives behind the words. Remember, a negotiator doesn't usually put his or her entire message into words. While the person's verbal message may convey honesty and conviction, his or her gestures, facial expressions, and tone of voice may convey doubt.

4. *Let your counterpart tell his or her story first.* Many salespeople have learned the value of this advice from the school of hard knocks. One printing salesperson told me of how he had once tried to impress a new prospect by saying his company specialized in two- and four-color printing. The prospect then told the salesperson that she would not be doing business with his printing company because her business had a need for usually one-color printing. The salesperson replied that his company obviously did one-color printing also, but the prospect had already made her decision. Had the salesperson let the prospect speak first, he would have been able to tailor his presentation to satisfy her needs and wants.

5. *Do not interrupt when your counterpart is speaking.* Interrupting a speaker is not good business for two reasons. First, it is rude. Second, you may be cutting off valuable information that will help you at a later point in the negotiation. Even if your counterpart is saying something that is inaccurate; let him or her finish. If you really listen, you should gain valuable information to serve as the basis of your next question.

6. *Fight off distractions.* When you are negotiating, try to create a situation in which you can think clearly and avoid interruptions. Interruptions and distractions tend to prevent negotiations from proceeding smoothly or may even cause a setback. Employees, peers, children, animals, and phones can all distract you and force your eye off the goal. If you can, create a good listening environment.

7. *Do not trust your memory.* Write everything down. Any time someone tells you something in a negotiation, write it down. It is amazing how much conflicting information will come up at a later time. If you are able to correct your counterpart or refresh his or her memory with facts and figures shared with you in an earlier session, you will earn a tremendous amount of credibility and power. Writing things down may take a few minutes longer, but the results are well worth the time.

8. *Listen with a goal in mind.* If you have a listening goal, you can look for words and nonverbal cues that add information you are seeking. When you hear specific bits of information, such as your counterpart's willingness to concede on the price, you can expand with more specific questions.

9. *Give your counterpart your undivided attention.* It is important to look your counterpart in the eye when he or she is speaking. Your goal is to create a win/win outcome so that your counterpart will be willing to negotiate with you again. Thus, your counterpart needs to think you are a fair, honest, and a decent person. One way to help achieve this goal is to pay close attention to your counterpart. Look the person in the eyes when he or she is speaking. What message are the eyes sending? What message is his or her nonverbal behavior sending? Many experienced negotiators have found that with careful attention they can tell what their counterpart is really thinking and feeling. Is he or she lying or telling the truth? Is the person nervous and desperate to complete the negotiation?

Careful attention and observation will help you determine your counterpart's true meaning.

10. *React to the message, not to the person.* As mentioned earlier, you want your counterpart to be willing to negotiate with you again. This won't happen if you react to the person and offend his or her dignity. It is helpful to try and understand *why* your counterpart says the things he or she does. Elaine Donaldson, a professor of psychology at the University of Michigan, says, "People do what they think they have to do in order to get what they think they want." This is true with negotiators. When we negotiate, we are trying to change a relationship. Your counterpart is trying to change it according to his or her best interests. If you were in your counterpart's shoes, you may do the same thing. If you are going to react, attack the message and not your counterpart personally.

11. *Don't get angry.* When you become angry, your counterpart has gained control in triggering your response. In the angry mode, you are probably not in the best frame of mind to make the best decisions. Emotions of any kind hinder the listening process. Anger especially interferes with the problem-solving process involved in negotiations. When you are angry, you tend to shut out your counterpart.

If you are going to get angry, do it for the effect, but retain control of your emotions so you can keep control of the negotiations. Remember when Nikita Khrushchev pounded his shoe on the table in the United Nations? The effect worked well for him.

12. *Remember, it is impossible to listen and speak at the same time.* If you are speaking, you are tipping your hand and not getting the information you need from your counterpart. Obviously, you will have to speak at some point so that your counterpart can help meet your needs and goals, but it is more important for you to learn your counterpart's frame of reference. With information on your counterpart, you will be in control of the negotiation. And when you are in control, you will be acting and your counterpart will be reacting; it is usually better to be the one in the driver's seat.

Interactive Listening Skills

The second type of listening skills are those used to *interact* with the speaker. These skills help ensure that you understand what the sender is communicating, and they acknowledge the sender's feelings. Interactive skills include clarifying, verifying, and reflecting.

Clarifying

Clarifying is using facilitative questions to clarify information, get additional information, and explore all sides of an issue. Examples: "Can you clarify this?" "What specific information do you want?" "When do you want the report?"

Verifying

Verifying is paraphrasing the speaker's words to ensure understanding and to check meaning and interpretation with him or her. Examples: "As I understand it, your plan is…" "It sounds like you're saying…" "This is what you've decided and the reasons are…"

Reflecting

Reflecting is making empathetic remarks that acknowledge the speaker's feelings. If negotiators are to create win/win outcomes, they must be empathetic. Most people think of themselves as relatively empathetic. In fact, most of us easily feel empathy for others who are experiencing what we have experienced. But true empathy is a skill, not a memory. Negotiators who have developed the ability to empathize can display it even when encountering counterparts with whom they have little in common. The ability of a negotiator to empathize has been found to significantly affect the counterpart's behavior and attitudes.

To be empathetic, negotiators need to accurately perceive the content of the message. Second, they need to give attention to the emotional components and the unexpressed core meanings of the message. Finally, they need to attend to the feelings of the other but remain detached, whereas a *sympathetic* individual would adopt those feelings as his or her own. Empathy involves understanding and relating to another's feelings. Examples: "I can see that you were frustrated because…" "You felt that you didn't get a fair shake." "You seem very confident that you can do a great job for…"

To truly practice reflective listening, you must make no judgments and pass along no opinions or provide any solutions. You simply acknowledge the sender's emotional content. Examples:

Sender: "How do you expect me to
                                 complete the project by next
                                 Monday?"

Reflective response: "It sounds like you are over-whelmed by your increased workload."

or

Sender: "Hey Mary, what's the idea of not approving my requisition for a new filing cabinet?"

Reflective response: "You sound really upset over not getting your request approved."

The goal of reflective listening is to acknowledge the emotion that your counterpart has conveyed and to reflect back the content using different words. Example:

Sender: "I can't believe you want me to do the job in less than a week."

Reflective response: "You sound stressed about the amount of time it will take to complete the job."

If your reflective response is constructed properly, the natural reaction from your counterpart will be to provide more explanation and information. Here are some key points you will find helpful in learning to be empathetic.

1. *Recognize and identify emotions.* Most inexperienced negotiators are not adept at recognizing the myriad emotions. You will find it easier to identify others' emotions if you can easily identify your own. Are you frustrated, stressed, angry, happy, sad, nervous?

2. *Rephrase the content.* If you restate your counterpart's comments word for word, he or she will believe you are parroting him or her. Doing so not

only sounds awkward, it will make your counter-part angry. The key is to restate the content using different words.

3. *Make noncommittal responses.* A good way to start reflective statements is with such phrases as "It sounds like..." "It appears that..." "It seems like..." These phrases work well because they are noncommittal. If you blatantly state, "You are angry because..." most people will proceed to tell you why you are incorrect.

4. *Make educated guesses.* Recently I was involved in a negotiation in which one negotiator told his counterpart that the other had submitted a ridiculous offer in an attempt to buy his company. The negotiator responded, "It almost sounds like you are insulted by my offer." The counterpart replied, "Not insulted, just shocked." Although the negotiator was not entirely accurate in his assessment of his counterpart's emotion, it was a good educated guess.

In conclusion, when you want to improve your listening skills, a good rule to remember is that God gave you two ears and one mouth—you should use them in their respective proportions. To succeed in negotiations, you must understand the needs, wants, and motivations of your counterpart. To understand those needs, you must hear. To hear, you must listen.

6

NONVERBAL BEHAVIOR: THE LANGUAGES OF NEGOTIATING

Researchers in nonverbal communications claim that as much as 90 percent of the meaning transmitted between two people in face-to-face communications is via nonverbal channels. This means that as little as 10 percent of your verbal communication will have an impact on the outcome of your negotiations. If these figures are even close to reality, then the importance of nonverbal negotiation skills cannot be underestimated.

Albert Mehrabian, a professor at the University of California, Los Angeles, found that only 7 percent of people's feelings and attitudes are communicated with words; 38 percent of feelings are communicated via tone of voice, and an amazing 55 percent through nonverbal behaviors.[4] What is staggering about these percentages is that the communication channel you have the most control over, the verbal, has the least impact on your counterpart. And the channels over which you have the least control, vocal intonation and nonverbal behavior, have the most impact.

It has also been documented that in a thirty-minute negotiation, two people can send over 800 different non-verbal messages. Think back to the last time you conducted a negotiation. What was the stance or sitting position of your counterpart? Did he or she maintain eye contact with you? Were the person's arms or legs crossed? If neither participant is aware or has an understanding of nonverbal behavior, both are communicating on a subconscious level. No wonder so many negotiations have a negative outcome!

The Three Stages of Nonverbal Negotiations

Learning the art of perceiving nonverbal communications is almost as difficult as acquiring fluency in a foreign language. In addition to studying your own gestures and the meaning you are conveying to your counterpart, you must also become aware of your counterpart's nonverbal behavior. As you become more experienced at recognizing various nonverbal communications, you will pass through three distinct stages.

Stage 1: Awareness of Your Counterpart

After some initial training, you will begin to notice nonverbal signs your counterpart is displaying. Is he or she talking to you with arms or legs crossed? Is he or she looking at you eyeball to eyeball? Is the person covering his or her mouth while speaking to you or asking a question? You will begin to recognize clusters of signals that will tell you whether your counterpart is honest, trustworthy, bored, angry, or defensive. At this stage, you are not 100 percent certain how to handle these signals, but you are aware that something is going on.

Stage 2: Awareness of Yourself

After you become aware that your counterpart is telling you things without opening his or her mouth, you begin to realize that you also are communicating nonverbally. On one of my sales calls, I became aware that the buyer was sitting back in his chair with both his legs and arms crossed.

When it hit me that he wasn't being receptive, I questioned my own behavior. Sure enough, I was sitting back in my chair, with my briefcase in my lap and my legs crossed.

Stage 3: Management of Self and Others Through Nonverbal Communications

In the example above, I quickly changed my own nonverbal communication. When I put my briefcase on the floor beside my chair, slid forward in my seat, and uncrossed my legs, the buyer slowly began to change his position to a much more receptive one. Being able to manage your nonverbal behavior and, in turn, to manage the nonverbal behavior of your counterpart, is the ultimate in nonverbal communication. Body language reflects people's true feelings. The better you can speak the language, the better you will be able to understand the true meaning and feelings of your counterpart.

Gestures Come in Clusters

Many skeptics have stated that it is difficult to tell what someone is thinking by singling out one gesture. Maybe you have heard a comment such as, "I am crossing my arms because I am cold, not because I am being defensive." The skeptics are somewhat right. A single gesture is like a word standing alone. It is difficult to understand out of context, and you cannot be sure of its true meaning. However, when gestures are fit together in clusters, they begin to take on some meaning that represents what is going on in your counterpart's mind. For example, someone who is not being honest or trustworthy would display a group of congruent gestures including a lack of eye contact, hands around the mouth, touching the face, and fidgeting.

The question usually arises, how accurate are non-verbal communications compared to verbal ones? D. A. Humphries, a British researcher, has found occasional dichotomies between obvious verbal and nonverbal meanings. After analyzing videotapes of conversations, he found that clusters of nonverbal gestures proved to be more accurate and truthful representations of each person's feelings.[5]

It will be difficult at first to be aware of nonverbal communications. But, like any language, if you study the nonverbal behavior of yourself and others on a daily basis, you will begin to recognize and understand the clustering process. Nonverbal communication is critical to negotiations because it lets you know when you must withdraw or do something different to obtain the outcome you desire.

When scanning a counterpart for clusters of gestures, a good formula to follow is to divide the body into five categories: the face and head, body, arms, hands, and legs.

The Face and Head

The face and head truly provide a window into your counterpart's soul. Here are some signs to look for:

- Someone who is trying to hide something will tend to avoid eye contact with you or break eye contact as he or she speaks untruthful words.
- Someone who is bored may gaze past you or glance around the room.
- Someone who is angry with you or feels superior may maintain piercing eye contact.
- Someone who is evaluating what you are saying may turn his or her head slightly to one side, almost as though wanting to hear you even better.

- Someone who is uncertain about what is being said may tilt his or her head slightly.
- Someone who is in agreement may nod his or her head as you are speaking.
- Someone who is being honest and trustworthy maintains good eye contact and will smile.

The Body

The body also plays an important role in nonverbal communication. If your counterpart is leaning closer to you, you are making positive progress. The more your counterpart likes you, the closer he or she will be willing to position his or her body. When you say or do things that your counterpart disagrees with, he or she will tend to position his or her body away from you. To create a win/win outcome, you should always position your body toward your counterpart.

Here are other signs to watch for:

- Someone who is interested and in agreement will usually lean toward you or position his or her body closer to you.

- Someone who is in disagreement with, uncertain about, or bored with what you are saying will generally turn his or her body away from you or lean back farther in his or her chair.

- Someone who moves from side to side, shifting his or her weight may feel insecure, nervous, or in doubt.

The Arms

Intensity is the key factor when monitoring the arms as a channel in nonverbal communication. In general, the more open the position of the arms, the more receptive your counterpart is to the negotiation process. If your counter-part's arms are folded tightly across his or her chest, prob-ably the person is not receptive to your communication.

The arms are one of the best indicators of changes in the nonverbal communication process. As you start the negotiation, your counterpart's arms may be resting in an open fashion on the table where you are both sitting. Then, when you mention that your company has a standard deposit of 50 percent on all first-time orders, the person may take his or her arms off the table and cross them over his or her chest. That would be a good indication that what you just said was not received well. Your words may need further clarification or, better yet, you should ask your counterpart whether he or she has a concern about the 50 percent deposit.

The Hands

Nonverbal signals from the hands can be divided into three main categories: presentation of the palms, self-touching gestures, and involuntary hand movements.

First, open palms are generally considered a positive nonverbal message. This goes back to medieval days. Showing your counterpart open palms indicates that you have no weapons and nothing to hide.

Second, self-touching gestures to the nose, chin, ear, arm, or clothing usually indicate that your counterpart is nervous and lacks confidence about what he or she is saying. Just watch any baseball game. Before the batter steps up to the plate or the pitcher throws the ball, both are likely to dispel their nervousness by touching their hat, uniform, face, or groin.

Third, the most revealing hand gestures are involun-tary hand movements. People have little ability to control their true feelings, which are commonly revealed through the hands.

The Legs

When asked why they cross their legs, most people will answer that they do so for comfort. Although they are being truthful, they are only partially correct. If you have ever crossed your legs for a long period of time, you know that this position can become painfully uncomfortable.

Crossing your legs can have a devastating effect on a negotiation. In a study described in *How to Read a Person Like a Book,* Gerard I. Nierenberg and Henry H. Calero found after videotaping 2,000 transactions that no sales were made by people who had their legs crossed.

If you want your counterpart to receive your message as being cooperative and trustworthy, you are better off if you do not cross your legs. With your legs uncrossed, your feet flat on the floor, and your body tilted slightly toward your counterpart, you will have a better chance of sending an open, positive signal.

How to Read Your Counterpart's Emotions

Dominance and Power
Feet on desk
Piercing eye contact
Hands behind head or neck
Hands on hips
Palm-down handshake
Standing while other is seated
Steepling (fingertips touching)

Submission and Nervousness
Fidgeting
Minimum eye contact
Hands to face, hair, etc.
Briefcase guarding body
Palm-up handshake
Throat clearing

Disagreement, Anger, and Skepticism
Red skin
Finger pointing
Squinting eyes
Frowning
Body turned away
Crossed arms or legs

Boredom and Lack of Interest
Lack of eye contact
Playing with objects on desk
Blank stare
Drumming on table
Picking at clothes
Looking at watch, door, etc.

Uncertainty and Indecision
Cleaning glasses
Look of puzzlement
Fingers to mouth
Biting lip
Pacing back and forth
Tilting head

Suspicion and Dishonesty
Touching nose while
   speaking
Covering mouth
Avoiding eye contact
Incongruity of gestures
Crossed arms or legs
Moving body away

Evaluation
Nodding
Eye squint
Good eye contact
Tilting head slightly
Chin stroking
Index finger to lips
Hands to chest

Confidence, Cooperation, and Honesty
Leaning forward in seat
Arms and palms open
Great eye contact
Feet flat on floor
Legs uncrossed
Move with counterpart's
   rhythm
Smiling

7

BUILDING TRUST IN NEGOTIATION

The more your counterpart trusts you, the easier you will find it to negotiate a win/win outcome. If for whatever reason your counterpart considers you untrustworthy, you will find it difficult to obtain even minor concessions. Think about it. If you don't trust someone, you will usually proceed very cautiously, not wanting to compromise for fear you will be a victim.

Here are some suggestions to help build trust with your counterpart:

1. *Do what you say you are going to do.* If you tell your counterpart you will discount the price 5 percent, then do so. Each time you do something you said you were going to do helps build trust with your counterpart.

2. *Go beyond the conventional relationship.* Recently I was involved in a contract negotiation. Because I was unfamiliar with the type of contract I was negotiating, I asked my counterpart if I could have more time to study the contract. His response was, "Of course." He then went on to ask me whether I would like samples of some of the competitors' contracts so I could compare them with what he was offering. By giving me these contracts to help educate me, he went well beyond the conventional

relationship. My trust in this counterpart went up quickly.

3. *Overcommunicate.* When negotiations get tough, the natural tendency is to communicate less. Resist the urge to stop communicating. Open and honest communication breeds trust.

4. *Be honest . . . when it costs you something to be honest.* If your counterpart has made a mistake in adding his figures, tell him. A client recently called and told me I had billed him less than I had quoted. This was true, because the client had switched the program I was doing from two half-days to one full day, for which I charge less. When I explained this to the client, he replied, "You didn't have to do that, it wasn't that much difference." My response was, "You didn't have to call me; maybe that's why we work well together."

5. *Be patient.* If you want to build trust with your counterpart, you will find it easier to do so if you are patient. Everyone has experienced a fast-talking salesperson who tells you every reason in the world why you need to make a decision immediately. Patience breeds trust and better decisions.

6. *Accept honest mistakes.* If you make a mistake in your calculations or decision making, admit it. Doing so goes a long way toward building both trust and credibility.

7. *Safeguard for fairness.* It is *your* responsibility to ensure that your counterpart gets a fair outcome. If you guard your character, your reputation as a negotiator will take care of itself.

8

SHARKS, CARP, AND DOLPHINS: YOUR NEGOTIATING COUNTERPARTS

When negotiating, it has been my experience that you will be dealing with one of three types of counterparts: sharks, carp, or dolphins. Each type has a different pattern and style of negotiating, and each will have a different response to your moves. In *The Strategy of the Dolphin*, Dudley Lynch and Paul L. Kordis shed light on how each of these three types of negotiators are likely to respond.[6]

The Shark

When asked, most people will agree they have negotiated with a shark. Sharks are the ones with the sharp teeth who are blinded by the attitude that there must be a winner and loser in every negotiation. Because sharks also believe in scarcity, they want to get as much as they can, in every case, regardless of the cost. Sharks also believe that because there must always be a loser, they must do anything to ensure it won't be them.

The shark's basic nature when negotiating is to *take over* or *trade off*. This is because the shark's desire is to beat his or her counterpart at all costs. But, if the shark's efforts to win are thwarted, he or she will resort to a more friendly trade-off strategy. Sharks only feel comfortable when they are in total control, and one of their specialties is to confuse their counterpart with crises and situations that force others to play their game. A second characteristic of sharks is to assume that they always have the best and only possible solution to the negotiation. The shark has a desperate need to be right 100 percent of the time and will go to any extreme to cover up his failures and shortcomings. Because a shark will even lie to support his shortcomings, you constantly need to be on guard when negotiating with a shark. One bad move and you will be eaten alive.

The overwhelming reason it is difficult to negotiate with sharks is that they lack the ability to be creative in their strategy. When a shark's takeover strategy fails, he or she becomes even more focused on "the kill." Instead of trying a different strategy, the shark does more of the same. The shark cannot think otherwise, because he or she has the determination to win at all costs, even when going up against the steepest odds.

The result of this strategy is that sharks have only two methods of dealing with any negotiation. They have no ability to try anything different or to learn from their mistakes. Their attitude of scarcity dictates their actions and reactions. If you are a shark, now is the time to sit back and learn from the dolphins, described later in this section.

The Carp

Neither carp nor sharks are well known in negotiating circles as brilliant dealmakers. In part, they are blinded by their view of the world. Like sharks, the carp believe that we live in a world of scarcity. Because of this belief, they do not expect to ever have enough. They walk into a negotiation feeling they cannot win. Believing this, they focus their efforts on not losing what they currently have.

When responding to external events, the "old brain" is said to provide us with the proverbial "three F's": fight, flight, or freeze. Normally, the carp will use only the latter two of these responses. If the carp negotiates with a shark or a dolphin, he will most likely be eaten alive. In fact, the carp even walks into the negotiation believing that he or she will be eaten alive. With this attitude, most carp will avoid, at all costs, making decisions or entering into a negotiation. They stay in the company of other carp because this is the only environment in which they feel safe.

Because carp do not like any type of confrontation, their normal responses are to *give in* or *get out*. Neither of these responses, when used repeatedly, leads to positive outcomes. If you repeatedly "get out" and avoid negotiations, you will become cut off and isolated from all except your fellow carp. These are the people who will go home with their ball and their bat, regardless of their age or the game they are playing. The "give in" strategy is even worse. In the worst case scenario, eventually you will have nothing else to give up and will be eaten alive.

Seldom does one side have all the power. If you are a carp, you need to concentrate on raising your level of aspiration. Research demonstrates that your aspiration level will dictate your outcome. If you let your past failures dictate your aspiration level, chances are you will even find it difficult to not lose what you already have.

The Dolphin

In *The Strategy of the Dolphin,* Lynch and Kordis chose the dolphin for comparison because of the animal's high intelligence and its ability to learn from experience. When dolphins do not get what they want, they quickly and precisely alter their behaviors in sometimes ingenious ways in pursuit of what they are after. In fact, dolphins, in their own way, may be more intelligent than we humans.

Dolphins, when confronted by a shark, have the reputation of repeatedly circling and ramming the shark with their bulbous noses. Using their noses as bludgeons, they methodically crush the shark's rib cage until the ferocious animal helplessly sinks to the bottom of the ocean.

As Lynch and Kordis state, "The strategy of the dolphin requires that we think about how we think." In negotiation, the dolphin has the ability to successfully adapt to any situation he or she encounters. If one strategy is unsuccessful, the dolphin is quick to learn and respond with a stream of possibilities. In the pool of life, the shark is usually successful at eating the carp and sometimes even other sharks. But seldom will a shark eat a dolphin. The dolphin is too intelligent and creative not to learn from his or her mistakes and the mistakes of others.

The major difference among the carp, shark, and dolphin is that the dolphin believes in both potential scarcity and potential abundance. Because dolphins believe they can have both, they learn to leverage what they have and use their resources superbly. Unlike dolphins, sharks and carp tend to view negotiations as a finite experience—that is, to take over, trade off, give in, or get out. All of these outcomes can be considered zero-sum games in which no new wealth is created. Instead, wealth is shifted around. Dolphins are different. They know that over time, all zero-sum strategies tend to degenerate into lose/lose strategies. The shark runs out of victims and trade-off players, and carp, using give-in strategies, end up with less and less.

Although we speak negatively of the shark's and carp's zero-sum strategies, there are some instances in which the dolphin will deliberately use a win/lose strategy. Dolphins will use zero-sum strategies as follows:

Take over when

- Time is limited or a specific outcome is crucial
- The relationship is of little importance and a specific outcome is critical
- Appropriate retaliation is necessary

Trade off when

- Time is short
- The issue is trivial
- One still cares about the relationship
- Others will not cooperate fully

Give in when

- The issue is trivial and the relationship is crucial
- It is wise to "buy time"
- The dolphin discovers he or she is wrong

Get out when

- The outcome does not matter much
- More pressing needs exist
- One needs to gather information
- Emotions need time to cool

Key Characteristics of Dolphins

Dolphins have four key characteristics:

1. *They play an infinite rather than a finite game.* Dolphins realize that negotiation does not happen in a vacuum. Every action they make in the negotiation will have a reaction. They realize that because the negotiation, like life, is an infinite game, they may have to deal with their counterpart in the future.

This realization increases the likelihood that cooperation and trust will enhance making the relationship more durable.

2. *They avoid unnecessary conflict by cooperating as long as the other players do likewise.* Dolphins realize that cooperation and trust are critical.

3. *They respond promptly to a "mean" move by retaliating properly.* Dolphins recognize the importance of responding quickly and appropriately when provoked. Putting off a response when you have been dealt an unjust blow invites being misunderstood. Whether the problem is your teenager testing your home curfew policy or your client altering the terms of your contract, delaying a response is sending the wrong signal, inviting more sharklike behaviors. Dolphins retaliate promptly to avoid being misunderstood.

4. *While quick to retaliate, dolphins are also quick to forgive.* If their counterpart shows any signs of cooperation, dolphins quickly switch to a more cooperative strategy.

In conclusion, sharks tend to spend the majority of their time trying to control their counterpart and expect to conclude the negotiation with a definite winner and loser. In contrast, dolphins spend the majority of their time building trust and rapport with their counterpart. They do so by discovering the true needs and wants of their counterpart. When the needs and wants of both counterparts are known, and there is an atmosphere of trust and cooperation, the possibility of creating a win/win outcome exists. This is the only outcome that produces a net gain in wealth for all parties involved.

Eighteen Rules of Negotiation

1. Assume that everything is negotiable.

2. Aim your aspirations high.

3. Never accept the first offer.

4. Deal from strength if you can, but create the appearance of strength, regardless.

5. Put what you have agreed on in writing.

6. Recognize that the other party is probably holding back valuable information.

7. Flinch to create doubt in the counterpart's mind and to add value to a concession.

8. Find out what your counterpart wants. Do not assume that his or her wants and needs are the same as yours.

9. Concede slowly and call a concession a concession.

10. Keep your counterpart in the dark about your strategy and your stake in the deal.

11. Try to get your counterpart to lower his or her level of aspiration.

12. Ask questions if you do not understand what is going on. Do not let your counterpart deliberately confuse you.

13. Answer questions with a question to avoid giving away information needlessly.

14. Invoke the higher authority to buy more time.

15. Information is power—get as much as possible.

16. Verify anything you are told that you do not know to be a fact.

17. Be cooperative and friendly. Avoid abrasiveness, which often breaks down negotiations.

18. Use the power of competition. Remember that power can be real or imaginary.

9

FIFTY STRATEGIES AND TACTICS FOR SUCCESSFUL NEGOTIATION

Following are fifty strategies and tactics commonly used by parties in negotiations. If you learn to identify them, you can use these strategies and tactics or be able to counter them, if necessary.

1. Principle of the Flinch

Successful negotiators have a habit of flinching. The flinch is communicated by making a sour look or a remark of disbelief any time one's counterpart mentions the price or conditions of his or her product or service. I used to think that the flinch was a rather silly tactic until I realized how effective it was when someone used it on me.

Example

Salesperson:	"The price of the brochures will be $3,000 for a quantity of 1,000."
Client (look of surprise):	"You've got to be kidding me. Why so much?"
Salesperson (naturally trying to add value to the price):	"Of course, that includes the copywriting, photography, typesetting, printing, varnish, and binding."

If the client did not flinch or act surprised, the salesperson would more likely use the "giveaways" from the flinch as additional costs:

Client:	"$3,000—I thought it would be a lot more than that."
Salesperson:	"Of course, that doesn't include the copywriting, photography, or varnish. Those will be added on to the base price."

Counter

When someone flinches at your price, defend your product on its own merit. Do not give concessions until you have a solid understanding of why the person flinched. Many people flinch because they lack knowledge of your product, service, or price. Inexperienced negotiators tend to give up much too much, and much too soon.

2. Principle of Walk Away Power

As emphasized earlier in this book, in any relationship the side with the least commitment to continuing the relationship will have the most power. If you have the ability to walk away from the bargaining table when the tide turns, you will have greater leverage.

Example

Recently my wife, Kathleen, bought a daybed for our daughter. It had been advertised on sale for $77. When she went to pay for the bed, the salesman told her there was an additional $25 delivery fee. Kathleen didn't want to pay the fee because she had arranged for me to pick up the bed in my company truck. Yet she left the store with the $25 delivery fee still on the bill, because the clerk said it was non-negotiable, whether the store delivered the bed or not. In fact, the clerk said that if the store did not charge the fee, it would lose money on the bed.

Kathleen went home and called two other outlets of the same store. To each one, she stated she wanted to buy the daybed advertised on sale, and she asked whether there would be any delivery charge if she picked it up herself. Both outlets said no. Armed with this information, she called the first store and requested to have the delivery charge removed, or she would cancel the transaction and take her business to another outlet. The store agreed.

One week later, when we went to pick up the bed, the clerk behind the counter stated that the person Kathleen had talked to did not have the authority to remove the delivery charge. After going back and forth, Kathleen finally said, "Just give me my $77 back and we'll buy the bed somewhere else." At this point, the clerk gave in and waived the fee.

If you are able to walk away, you will always retain the ability to create a win/win outcome.

Counter

If other people are interested in your product or service or if you can find a desired product or service elsewhere and still meet your goals, let your counterpart walk. If you chase the person down and bring him or her back to the bargaining table, your power will deteriorate considerably. Car salespeople are notorious for walking after customers when they walk away from dealing on a new car. Remember, if you keep walking, the leverage will be on your side…provided you have a way of contacting your counterpart again.

3. Principle of Competition

In most businesses, the power of competition can be devastating. Competition forces the seller to justify everything, and in some instances, to give away more than he or she planned. Sometimes the very threat of competition is enough to force concessions.

Example

Client: "I have gotten three bids and yours is $500 higher than the other two. I would really like to work with you if you can do something with your price."

Counter

Defend your price on the merits of quality and service. Once I was out on a sales call with a seasoned veteran who responded to the client's price question by stating as a matter of fact, "Mrs. Jones, my price is higher than the competition's because I am the one who is going to do the job right." It was so confidently stated that he convinced me and he convinced the client.

Be aware that many clients will tell you that your price is too high just to get rid of you. They have no intentions of working with you, even if you do lower your price.

4. Principle of the Written Policy

Whenever you reach an agreement with anyone, *you* should be the one to put it in writing. When you are the one to write the deal points, you can tie down all the loose ends that surround the issues that were agreed upon.

Example

You agree to lease office space from a building owner and the deal points are as follows:

- Two-year lease
- Lease rate of $3,000 per month for 4,000 square feet
- Two months free rent

After the handshake, the party who puts the terms in writing has the opportunity to tie down loose ends. For example:

- Two-year lease commencing on September 1, 1994.
- Lease rate will be $3,000 per month for 4,000 square feet but on a gross basis, not triple net. (The difference between these small words can add up to hundreds of dollars each month. On a gross rent, the landlord pays all extra costs such as taxes, garbage removal, cleaning fees, etc.)
- The two months free rent will start from the September 1 move-in date. (Most landlords like to put the free rent in the middle or at the end of the lease.)

Counter

If you do not agree with how your counterpart has tied up the loose ends in a written agreement, you should immediately fax or write back explaining how you feel the issues should be handled. If you do not respond immediately, you will lose tremendous bargaining power when you finally sit down at the negotiation table.

5. Principle of Low- or Highballing

In low- or highballing, someone makes a ridiculously low or high offer.

Example

You are trying to sell your house for $189,000. Your agent brings you an offer of $160,000 from a couple who saw the house over the weekend. If your house is competitively priced, this would be considered a lowball offer.

Lowballing is effective because it tends to lower a counterpart's aspirations. If you counter back at $180,000, the next offer of $175,000 would not seem so bad. If the counterpart had originally offered $175,000, you would have probably countered higher than $180,000.

Counter

If someone lowballs you, you can choose from three options:

1. Do not counter!

2. Counter back your asking price.

3. Counter back higher than your asking price. Tell the person that he or she misunderstood the actual price. This counters the ridiculous with the ridiculous.

4. Counter back at your original asking price, but state exclusions from your original offer.

If someone highballs you, there are three other options:

1. Do your homework to know whether the price is competitive.

2. Unleash the competition. Demonstrate with a competitive analysis that the price is unreasonably high.

3. Ask for a price breakdown.

6. Principle of the Higher Authority

Lacking the final say in a situation can create a very powerful position. In this situation, the negotiator has to go to someone else to gain final approval. More often than not, I have seen an experienced negotiator work the best deal he or she could, then run off to a higher authority. Usually, the negotiator will come back from the higher authority with instructions for an even better deal.

Example

A president of a corporation works the best deal he can on a piece of machinery. The initial price of the equipment was $450,000. He gets the salesperson to concede to a price of $428,000 with three months of use before the first payment. The president agrees to the deal but says he needs to take it to his board of directors for final approval.

The president comes back from the board of directors with the approval to sign the contract but at not more than $425,000. He even apologizes to the salesperson for the board's being so tough. The salesman gives in. In this case, the board may have been real or apparent. One of my students shared this example with me and dubbed the principle "the $3,000 tactic." It worked for him. Best of all, he *was* the board of directors, lock, stock, and barrel.

Counter

The best way to keep the principle of the higher authority from being used on you is to ask your counterpart in the very beginning whether he or she is the person who makes the final decision. If not, ask to make your presentation to the final decision maker. In the example, it may have been advantageous for the salesperson to negotiate the best possible outcome, then turn the negotiation over to his sales manager to see whether the manager could improve the outcome.

Counter to the Counter

If someone should ask if you are the final decision maker and you are not, be honest and say so. Then proceed to tell the counterpart that the final decision maker *always* listens to you and *always* takes your recommendations. Since your superior is impossible to get time with, it is in your counterpart's best interest to make his or her proposal to you.

After you obtain your best deal, you take it to the higher authority. Then you come back and say in disbelief, "This is the first time the higher authority has not gone with my recommendation. He said unless I can get the purchase price below $420,000, I cannot sign the contract. I really am sorry to put you through this when we thought we had a deal."

This tactic may cause ethical dissonance for some people. It is included because it has been used against me.

Counter to the Counter to the Counter

You have three options:

1. Practice the principle of the absurd. (#24)
2. Use the principle of tightening the screw (#20).
3. Walk away.

7. Principle of the Trial Balloon

Many times, you will want to find out how firm your counterpart is on the key issues. By sending up a trial balloon, you can judge his or her reaction to your proposal. Doing so will give you a better understanding when you get down to do the final negotiation.

Example

A seller is asking $150,000 for his house. As the buyer, you might ask: "If I could give you $130,000 in cash, and have the money to you in one week, would you be willing to sell your house at that price?" The seller says she will not sell for $130,000, but if you could come up with $140,000 she would be willing to sell the house. Now you know that when you do your final negotiations, in the worst case the buyer will take $140,000. This may or may not be with the all-cash buyout in one week, as you first described.

The trial balloon can also be used in the opening session of a negotiation. Recently I bought a used car for a friend. He had only $2,000 to spend. I surprised him by looking through the want ads and calling about cars in the $2,300 to $2,900 range.

I told each seller that I had only had $2,000 to spend and I wanted to know if that was even close enough for me to come over and take a look at the car. Some said no. Some said yes, that $2,000 was a possibility. And some said that they would not take $2,000 but that they would take $2,100. Knowing such information going into a negotiation changes your opening offer.

Counter

If someone sends a trial balloon into your arena, respond with shock or disbelief: "You're not serious, are you?" A second counter is to respond simply by saying, "That's not good enough." A third counter that may help restore leverage is to justify the worthiness of your car. You might state, "After seeing the car, I am confident you will agree that it's a bargain at $2,500."

Counter to the Counter

Justify your trial balloon. Sometimes, with the right explanation, your trial balloon will be filled with more than just hot air. If you can justify your position, you may be able to get your counterpart to change his or her initial point of reference.

8. Principle of the Extra or Add On

This principle comes into play after you have reached an initial deal. After you have reached what your counterpart thinks is an agreement, you place a condition on the final sale. The condition is the extra or add on.

Example

Buyer: "I will buy the car for $14,000, if you will upgrade the stereo and apply the sealant to the exterior paint."

Counter

Seller: "You are asking for something that makes my job more difficult. I have given you my very best price and now you are asking for something more. I could give you an upgraded stereo and the paint sealant, but that would have to be on the model with the smaller engine." Do not give up something major without getting something in return.

9. Principle of the Salami

Few people eat a whole salami with one swallow. Most have to cut it into small pieces. It just goes down easier that way. The same principle applies to negotiation. Major concessions are made with less resistance when they are cut into small pieces.

Example

You are in the market for a new stereo, cassette player, and compact disc player. The total system retails for $850. You have set a goal to purchase the system for $700. If you walked up to a salesperson and said you would take the system if he or she could sell it for $700, the salesperson would probably tell you to get lost. You stand a much higher chance of getting the system at your price if you use the salami technique.

First ask the salesperson what kind of discount he or she would give you if you purchased all three components at the same time. Maybe you could get a 10 percent discount off the total price.

Next ask the salesperson if he or she would take another $50 off if you took the floor model.

Finally, mention that you will buy the equipment right now if the salesperson will throw in the extended warranty on the compact disc player.

Before you know it, those little concessions will add up to $150.

Counter

There are several counters you can use when you think you are getting the salami.

First, you can expose the salami. Tell the person that you have made concession after concession and the negotiation is no longer a win/win affair.

Second, you can blow up. When your counterpart asks for his or her next slice, act as though this is the straw that broke the camel's back. Express disbelief that your counterpart has asked for another concession.

Third, you can counter with your own salami: "I will give you the extended warranty on the compact disc player if you will buy the extended warranty on the stereo and the cassette player for a period of three years." I have found that when you counter a salami with a salami, your counterpart will stop using this tactic.

10. Principle of the Non-negotiable Demand

Every once in a while you will run into someone who will say that an issue is non-negotiable. Union negotiators are famous for this.

People will say that something is non-negotiable for several reasons. First, it shows that they have strong convictions about the issue. Second, it tends to lower the level of their counterpart's expectations. Third, it forces the counterpart to reevaluate his or her position. And fourth, many times the counterpart will back off and bite into another issue.

Example

You are in the market to purchase a home. You find the home of your dreams and offer the seller $7,500 less than the asking price. The seller responds that his price is non-negotiable. Take it or leave it.

Counter

First, get your real estate agent (or any other third party/mediator) to try and reason with the seller. Second, use your walk-away power. If the seller gets no other bites, he may come looking for you. This happens many times when reality hits the seller and he realizes that his price is too high.

Recently, I stayed for a week at a hotel in Atlanta, Georgia. The hotel informed me that I had received a fax from my office and that there was a $5 charge for receiving the fax. Since I was going to be sending and receiving many faxes during the week, I asked to have the receiving fax charges waived. The person at the front desk told me it was hotel policy and the charges were non-negotiable. I asked to see the manager, who also told me the charges were non-negotiable. I then informed the manager that I would be moving to the hotel across the street for the rest of the week since they didn't charge for receiving faxes. The manager went to the general manager and gained approval for me to receive faxes at no charge.

Last, you can use the salami approach. Chisel away at the price, a little slice at a time. You may be able to get the seller to pay part of your closing costs or to carry back a second mortgage at a low interest rate. A piece at a time, you may be able to whittle away at what were believed to be non-negotiable issues.

11. Principle of Funny Money

This principle involves breaking dollars and cents into such small amounts that your counterpart doesn't realize he or she is dealing with large sums of money.

Example

Several years ago, a knife salesperson rang my doorbell and gave me a demonstration of cutlery I will never forget. When she had finished cutting up everything in my kitchen, I made the mistake of asking her how much the knives cost.

Her reply: "Peter, these knives have a full guarantee for a period of ten years. Over those ten years, they are only going to cost you about eighteen cents a day."

What this salesperson did was to break down the $633 total price into the daily cost. Even back then, I could afford eighteen cents a day. I still kick myself for falling for the funny money close.

Counter

Do your homework and spend your energy working out the total price figure. Car dealerships are the masters of using the funny money approach. They try to get the buyer to deal in the monthly payment and not the total price when they are negotiating. The dealers try to leave the buyer in the dark regarding the total price and interest rate until the deal has been struck.

Be willing to walk away if your counterpart is not willing to provide full disclosure of all terms.

12. Principle of Splitting the Difference

When two parties are still apart on an issue and the negotiation seems to be at a stalemate, one can offer to split the difference with the other counterpart.

Example

You are selling your car and do not want to come down any further than $2,000. The buyer doesn't want to pay any more than $1,800. Since you are $200 apart, either of you could offer to split the difference ($200 divided by 2) and do the deal for $1,900.

The rule of thumb in this situation is to let your counterpart offer to split the difference. If you offer to split the difference, your counterpart knows you are willing to lower your aspirations. A good solution is to state, "We are only $200 apart, what should we do?"

Counter

If the seller offered to split the difference, you know he or she is willing to accept $1,900. With this new information, you, as the buyer, could counter, "You have just stated that you are willing to take $1,900 for your car. I am willing to give you $1,800. That makes us only $100 apart. Why don't we split the difference and do the deal for $1,850?"

13. Principle of the Trade-off Concession

A good rule to remember in negotiation is to get something in return every time you give up something to your counterpart. Clearly, after you give up a deal point, it has very little value at a later time in the negotiation.

Example

Buyer: "I will buy your house for $180,000, but you will have to throw in your refrigerator, washer, and dryer for that price."

Seller: "I will throw in my refrigerator, washer, and dryer, but if I do that, you will have to close escrow in 30 days" or "I will throw in my refrigerator, washer, and dryer, but the price will have to be $182,000."

Counter

If you do not get something in return, here is (most likely) what will happen.

> Buyer: "I will buy your house for $180,000, but you will have to throw in your washer, dryer, and refrigerator for that price."
>
> Seller: "O.K."
>
> Buyer: "I will do the deal like we just agreed upon, but you will have to carry back a $20,000 second trust deed for a period of one year."
>
> Seller: "Wait a moment. I just gave you my washer, dryer, and refrigerator and now you want me to carry back a $20,000 second?"
>
> Buyer: "Why are you bringing up the washer, dryer, and refrigerator? We already agreed to that. The only thing we are discussing now is the $20,000 second trust deed."

Always get something in return. Otherwise you will get the big salami.

14. Principle of Apparent Withdrawal

There are times when you do not want to go to the extreme of walking away, but you do want to give your counterpart the feeling you are not committed to the deal. Apparent withdrawal should be used when you want to give the appearance that you do not care when in reality you want to retain control of the situation.

Example

Several years ago, a friend of mine was in negotiations to buy a beautiful home. He had gone through several days of negotiating on many deal points. He was in love with the house but the seller's last concession was still $4,000 above what he wanted to pay.

So my friend called the seller's broker and told her that he was going to have to withdraw from buying the house because he could not make the numbers work to his satisfaction. My friend was confident that neither the seller nor the broker would let a $300,000 deal go over $4,000. Since my friend was willing to pay the $4,000 if he had to, this is a case of apparent withdrawal.

Counter

First, you could walk away. Second, you could try to split the difference. Third, you could use a trade-off concession.

15. Principle of the Withdrawn Offer

There are times when it is in your best interest to withdraw your initial offer. This technique can be used when you feel you are being taken advantage of or are being put into a situation where you can only lose.

Example

Several years ago, I was selling a house that I owned with a partner. The asking price was $126,000. We had a buyer who was one of the toughest negotiators I have ever met. By using the salami, he reduced the price to $121,000, had extended the escrow to 90 days, and had gotten us to agree to carry back a $20,000 second mortgage at 9 percent. We thought the deal was finalized; then the buyer brought his wife into the picture.

The buyer's wife stated that she hated the kitchen and would not allow her husband to pay any more than

$119,000 for the house. That is when I told the buyer that I had bad news for him. My partner had decided that he would not sell the house for any less than $123,000. Since the buyer really did want the house, he spent the rest of his negotiating energy trying to get the price back down to $121,000.

Counter

First, you can walk away from the deal. If your counterpart is really serious, he or she will come back. Second, you can use apparent withdrawal. This is when you give the appearance that you are quitting but you really are in control of the situation.

16. Principle of the Alternative Close

The alternative close can be used when you have several alternatives that are acceptable to you. Salespeople are trained to use this approach to gain the commitment of the buyer.

Example

"I am willing to buy your new Honda Accord for $14,000 at 10 percent or at 11 percent. However, at 11 percent you have to throw in the paint sealant, upgraded stereo, and floor mats. Either way, the choice is yours."

Counter

First, you can say no to either deal and start over. Second, you can counter either deal. Third, you can use apparent withdrawal. Fourth, you can walk away. Fifth, you could use a trade-off concession.

17. Principle of the Decoy

With the decoy technique, you make a big issue of something that you really don't care much about. You are really after something else more important to you.

Example

You are buying a new copier and you strike a deal. The only option the copier does not have is the ability to collate documents, which the dealer agrees to install for you. When you were getting ready to sign the papers, the dealer informs you that it will take a month to get the copier ready and the collating feature installed. Although the time frame is not that important to you, you made a big issue of it in hopes that the dealer will make another price concession. In fact, you even tell the dealer you will go somewhere else if he cannot make the long wait worth your while.

Counter

First you can try to uncover the real motive. Second, you can use apparent withdrawal. Third, you can walk away.

18. Principle of the Dead Fish

The idea behind the dead fish principle is that you place something on the bargaining table that you do not expect to achieve and that you know your counterpart is going to object to like the smell of a dead fish. Although you do not care about the issue, when your counterpart makes a stink about it, you offer to give it up but turn it into a major concession on your part and get something in return.

Example

You are buying a used car from a private party. The seller is asking $2,000. You want to pay less, so you lay a dead fish on the table in the form of asking the seller to purchase new tires. You let the seller know that you are willing to drop the new tires demand, but he will have to lower his price by $300.

Counter

First, say the price is non-negotiable. Second, use apparent withdrawal. Third, walk away. Fourth, use the trade-off concession. You are willing to give a full power train warranty but that would require a price increase of $500.

19. Principle of Playing Stupid

There are times in life when it pays to play stupid. In other words, there are times when dumb is smart and smart is dumb. The power behind this principle is that people will help you more when they think you are handicapped by a lack of skills, knowledge, or information.

Example

Last year I was in the market for a new refrigerator. Wanting to make a good investment, I went to six different stores looking at three different brands of refrigerators. At about the fourth store, I began to realize that I knew more about the models than the salesmen who were waiting on me. Because too much knowledge would intimidate the salespersons and cause them to keep their guard up, I began to play stupid by telling them I had never bought a refrigerator before. I didn't volunteer the fact that I had already shopped at several other stores. When a salesperson had concluded his presentation, I narrowed the focus to the model I was interested in and told the salesperson that if he could sell me that refrigerator for $950, I would make the purchase right there and not even check at another store. This was $70 off his asking price and $135 off the lowest price I had found at the other stores. The salesman responded, "I can't give it to you for $950, but I can let you have it for $980." It was still a great deal.

On a side note, don't tell someone with whom you're negotiating that you've taken a course or workshop in negotiations. The last thing I ever share with anyone is that I teach a course in negotiations at San Diego State University. If I were to do that, my counterpart would bring extra ammunition.

Counter

Keep your guard up. You must realize at all times that any information you yield in a negotiation may be used against you at a later time. It is good to help a stupid person, but it is devastating to help a smart one dig your own grave.

20. Principle of Tightening the Screw

The idea behind the principle of tightening the screw is very simple. When someone makes you an offer that you think could be improved, you simply respond, "That's not good enough." Once you make the remark, pause, and let your counterpart make the next response.

Example

Henry Kissinger was a master at tightening the screw. It is reported that on one occasion his chief of staff wrote a report on an aspect of foreign policy. When the chief gave the report to his boss, Kissinger responded, "Is this your best work?" The chief thought for a moment and stated, "Mr. Kissinger, I think I can do better." So Kissinger gave him the report back. Two weeks later, the chief turned in the revised report. Kissinger kept it for a week and sent it back with a note attached saying, "Are you sure this is your best work?" Realizing that something must have been missing, the chief once again rewrote the report. This time he personally handed it to his boss and said, "Mr. Kissinger, this is my best work." Hearing that, Kissinger replied, "Then, this time I will read your report."

Counter

First, you can ask your counterpart, "If my offer is unacceptable, what do you consider acceptable?" The reason for asking this question is that you do not want to give away anything you do not have to. Many times people will tighten the screw just to get you to reevaluate your offer. In fact, some people tighten the screw religiously on every first offer.

Second, you can walk away. Third, you can play dumb is smart and smart is dumb.

21. Principle of Feel, Felt, and Found

The principle of feel felt, and found is one that has been transferred from the world of sales training. It is effective in helping your counterpart to understand your point of view.

Example

Buyer: "I can't believe you're asking $3,000 for this XYZ Brand copier."

Seller: "I can understand how you feel about the price. Many other XYZ owners have felt the same way until they found out how trouble-free and long lasting XYZ's are. There really is a difference, and that is what makes this price such a great value."

Counter

First, you can use the principle of turning the screw. Tell the seller that $3,000 is simply too much. Then pause. Second, you can use the principle of the higher authority. Your wife, husband, or business partner will only let you spend $2,800. Third, you could use the principle of the trade-off concession. Tell the seller that you will pay the $3,000 if he or she will throw in toner, chemicals, and service for one year.

22. Principle of Association

The principle of association is better referred to as "you will get your reward in heaven." The way this principle works is to tell someone that if they can meet your demands, you will reward them with something at a later date.

Example

I once called on an experienced printing buyer. When I reviewed the job he wanted me to give him a quote on, he made a point of telling me how much printing he was going to be purchasing down the road. Naturally, when I quoted the job I gave him a fair price because I wanted his future business. When I called him back with the quote, the buyer replied that he really wanted to use me but my price was higher than he had expected. The buyer stated, "If you can reduce the price 500 more dollars on this job, I will give you all my future work." Hence, I would be getting my reward in heaven.

Counter

My experience has led me to believe that you seldom get the reward that was promised you. Unfortunately, most people fall for this tactic when it is used on them. My advice is to tell your counterpart that your company does not allow you to discount a job on the promise of future business and that quotes are handled on a per-job basis.

A second counter that may be effective in this situation is to fight fire with fire. Tell your counterpart that you are not able to discount this job but, if he gives you this job, you will work on discounting another job in the future.

A third counter is to use the principle of standard practice. Simply state that it is not your company's policy to discount first time jobs.

Experienced negotiators have been burned by this technique too many times. Please, spare yourself the frustration of not getting the reward.

23. Principle of the Puppy Dog

The power behind the puppy dog principle lies in letting your counterpart have the object you are negotiating about before you consummate the deal. The principle derives its name from pet store owners who ask you to hold and play with little puppies while considering buying one. I ended up with a $400 Old English sheepdog because of this very tactic. With Sir Bentley licking me on the face, $400 seemed quite reasonable.

Example

Several years ago, my business partner and I bought a used boat. When we got stuck on the price, the owner suggested we take the boat to Catalina for the weekend. At the end of the weekend, he was convinced that we would feel the boat was worth the full $30,000 he was asking. When we returned from a great weekend, we still tried to get him to sell the boat for $28,000. At that point, the owner said he was confident he could find another buyer who would pay the full price. The owner was a smart man. He knew that after our great weekend in Catalina, we had already bought the boat in our minds. We would have paid $32,000 if he had raised the price over the weekend.

Counter

The principle of the puppy dog is so powerful, the only effective counter is to walk away. If you still want to negotiate, remove yourself and let a third party negotiate for you. Once your emotions have committed you, and your counterpart knows it, you are in a very vulnerable position.

24. Principle of the Absurd

Every once in a while, it will pay you to do something crazy—something so irrational that your counterpart will concede just to get rid of you. To make this technique effective, you have to do something that is far afield from how a rational person would go about solving the problem.

Example

Once at the Department of Motor Vehicles, I observed a woman who was so upset about having waited in three different lines and finding no one who could solve her problem that she began crying and screaming that all she wanted was someone who would treat her like a human being. When this outburst started, a manager took her aside and personally helped her sort out her registration problems.

A classic example of this principle was Soviet leader Nikita Khrushchev's banging a shoe on the table to emphasize a point at a meeting of the United Nations. What was interesting about this incident is that years later someone enlarged a photo of Khrushchev banging his shoe and noted that he still had both shoes on his feet. Either he had brought an extra shoe in his briefcase for the effect or he had a comrade pass him a shoe. Regardless, the absurd worked!

Counter

First, do not take the person's behavior personally. Many negotiators do the absurd just for the effect. Second, you can always walk away until your counterpart agrees to be reasonable. Third, when someone becomes unreasonable, use the principle of the withdrawn offer. If the person realizes that every time he or she becomes unreasonable, you withdraw the last offer you already agreed to, the person will realize this behavior is costly.

25. Principle of the Assumptive Close

The assumptive close is another principle that has been borrowed from the world of sales. The foundation of this principle is to make an offer and assume that your counterpart will take it.

Example

You are asking $300,000 for your house. You have stated that you would consider taking less if the escrow is short, but you haven't specified how much less. The buyer states he will buy the house for $270,000 and asks you if you want a fifteen- or a thirty-day escrow.

Counter

First, you could use the principle of the absurd. Blow up and get the price back to a respectable figure. Second, you could use the trade-off concession. You could say that you will accept the price of $270,000 if the buyer will pay all cash and pay it tomorrow. Third, you could come up with a higher price and split the difference. Fourth, you could walk away.

26. Principle of the Water Over the Dam

This principle originated with Roger Dawson, a superb speaker on negotiations. Once water flows over the dam, it is impossible to get it back. Similarly, once you have given up a deal point, it holds very little value at a future point in the negotiations.

Example

You want to buy a new copier for your office. In your initial meeting, the copier salesperson says that the price is $22,500. You mention that if he would throw in an extended maintenance contract, you would consider buying from him. The salesperson agrees.

At your next meeting, you tell the salesperson you would like to do business with him, but another manufacturer has agreed to add a feature that will enable you to do color copies. If the salesperson would agree to add that feature, you would be willing to buy the copier from him. The salesperson agrees. Now, all you have to do is get your boss's approval.

On your last meeting, you tell the salesperson that your boss has agreed but said you could not spend more than $20,000. If the salesperson can sell the machine for $20,000, you will buy the copier from him.

The salesperson says that he has already given up the extended warranty and the color copy feature, and now you are asking him to lower the price. He feels he has given more than his share and now you are asking for more.

Counter

The best counter is to remember the trade-off concession. Every time you give up something, get something in return. If you do not, the deal point you gave up will have very little value at a future point in time.

27. Principle of the Porcupine

When someone lays an issue on the table, it is a good idea to verify or test it. Good negotiators test everything their counterpart tells them for validity by treating it like a porcupine. The principle behind this issue is that if someone tossed you a porcupine, you would want to toss it back to them as quickly as possible.

Example

You are a copier salesperson and the copier you are selling costs $25,000.

When you tell your customer the price, she says her company cannot pay any more than $22,500 for a copier.

You say, "If I could show you the copier that would meet all your needs, and if I could prove to you that this copier is the most cost-effective in the long run, then would consider paying slightly more than $22,500?"

It has been my experience that when you use the porcupine, many people will reevaluate their demands.

Counter

First, you could counter with the higher authority and blame it on bosses or others with decision-making power. Second, you could try to give your counterpart a reward in heaven. Third, you could toss the porcupine right back at him or her.

28. Principle of the Good Guy/Bad Guy Technique

The good guy/bad guy technique is very similar to the principle of the higher authority but is much more specific. With good guy/bad guy, one person pretends to be on your side and appears to help you make the deal. But every time you strike a deal, the good guy marches off to the bad guy for final approval. Naturally, the bad guy will renegotiate the deal you have worked out with the good guy.

Any time you get into this scenario, you can end up with devastating consequences if you do not expose the technique.

Example

If you have ever bought a new car, most likely you have experienced the frustration of being in a good guy/bad guy situation. After you and the salesperson have test-driven the car, the salesperson takes you into the closing room to draw up the initial deal. Since the salesperson cannot approve anything himself, he marches off to the sales manager to get the manager's input on the deal. It is the job of the sales manager to rewrite the deal to get more money for the dealership. Then, the salesperson will return and say that you are close, but the original deal will not work. What is scary is that dealerships go through this process whether your offer is a good one or a bad one.

Counter

First, you can fight fire with fire. The last time I bought a new car, I took my wife. Every time the salesperson went off to the sales manager, I took my deal to my wife (who was in the lobby) to review it. Then, when we came back into the closing room, the salesperson told me that we had a deal, but they had to raise the price of the car $500. When the salesperson told me that, I replied that now we really had two problems because my wife had said I couldn't do the deal at the previous price unless I could get the interest rate down another point.

Second, you can expose this technique. Tell your counterparts that they are using good guy/bad guy and you do not appreciate it. One time I became so angry that I told the salesperson that if he did not have enough authority to make the deal then to bring in someone who could. I told him the next time he left the room, I would leave also. If the salesperson needs to get approval from the sales manager, he can call him on the phone with you in the room.

29. Principle of Brinkmanship

The principle of brinkmanship involves pushing your counterpart right up to the edge of some terrible outcome, then threatening to push. Usually both sides have a great deal to lose if the negotiations fail and a great deal to win if they succeed.

Example

Lee Iacocca, as chairman of Chrysler Corporation, used brinkmanship when he was negotiating with the auto unions. Iacocca's goal was to have the unions accept a package at $17 per hour. The union would not settle for any less than $20 per hour. One bitter night, Iacocca addressed the union negotiating committee. "It was one of the shortest speeches I have ever given," he recalls. "You've got until morning to make a decision. If you don't help me out, I'm going to blow your brains out. I'll declare bankruptcy in the morning and you'll all be out of work. You've got eight hours to make up your minds. It's up to you."[7]

In this example, Iacocca practiced brinkmanship by forcing the unions to the edge of the cliff and then threatening to push. Although the unions did concede, the Chrysler story has turned out to be a win/win for everyone: the workers, the government, the company, and most of all Lee Iacocca.

Counter

When someone practices brinkmanship against you, you have three choices. First, if you believe your counterpart has the power to back up his or her threat, you can walk away and accept the consequences. Second, you can give in and try to negotiate other deal points. Third, you can give your counterpart the appearance of giving in and concede in hopes of renegotiating the major issues.

30. Principle of the Scrambled Eggs

The principle of the scrambled eggs is used when counterparts want to intentionally confuse you. Sometimes they will do it with facts and figures, sometimes they will do it with false information. Either way, their hope is to confuse your decision-making process.

Example

A salesperson was adding up the cost of some furniture. The buyer told him she did not want to spend more than $3,000 for the four pieces of furniture. He added up the prices and the total came to only $2,800. It looked like they had a winner. When the buyer and seller went to do the paperwork at the sales counter, the salesman re-added the figures and discovered he had made a $200 error. When he added tax, delivery fees, and the correct figures, he was well over the buyer's $3,000 budget.

A second example is for someone to use facts, such as Kelly Bluebook prices, to establish a value on something. The person will share with you the bottom-line figures, hoping to create more support for his or her side and that you don't ask for proof or a breakdown.

Counter

First, you can expose the fact that the figures are not correct. Second, you could expose the fact that you think the person was trying to deceive you. Third, you could ask for verification and proof. Fourth, you could walk away.

31. Principle of the False Alarm

Have you ever been involved in a negotiation and thought that you had concluded a deal, only to learn that the other person was just getting his or her negotiations started? This is known as the principle of the false alarm.

Example

You are selling your car and negotiate with a buyer for about thirty minutes. Finally, you agree to drop your price by $300. At last, you think you have a deal. Then the buyer tells you that before he can actually buy the car, he needs to have his wife come over and drive it.

Counter

First, when he comes back with his wife, you could use the principle of the withdrawn offer. Tell him you shared the deal with your significant other and he or she will not let you deduct the $300 from the price. This also employs the principle of the higher authority.

Second, you could expose this tactic and tell the buyer that the deal you just struck is good only now. If he does not take this deal, you will have to start the negotiations over. Third, you could walk away.

32. Principle of Flattery or Humor

One effective way to gain leverage in a negotiation is to use flattery or humor. This works because when humor is used effectively, it has the impact of relaxing the negotiating parties. When flattery is used effectively, it has the impact of motivating the counterpart to respond.

Example

A president of a nonprofit corporation called and asked if I was willing to speak at the organization's annual dinner. In his opening comment the president stated, "Although I do not have a budget to pay you, I need a great speaker and you are the best I know." With this type of flattery, and in this case a very worthy cause, it was hard to say no.

Counter

If the flattery is sincere, it is important to acknowledge your appreciation. It is also important to be able to set the flattery aside and counter back on the importance or value of your product or service. A second counter is to negotiate something that has a value other than money. In this specific situation, I negotiated for an advertisement in their fund raising program.

33. Principle of Setting a Limit

It is common knowledge that the Pareto principle is alive and well in the business of negotiations. As noted earlier, this principle states that most negotiations will be finalized in the last 20 percent of time available. Limits are set by either party in just about every form imaginable. They could include limits on price, either high or low, limits on time, limits on geography, or limits on communication.

It is important to realize that if the other side sets limitations, you do not have to accept them. In fact, it is a good idea to question all limitations your counterpart sets. On the other hand, it is a good idea to have your own limits set before you go into a negotiation. These guidelines serve as your goals.

Example

You make an offer to buy a house. The seller counters back $2,000 higher than the last offer, giving you only twenty-four hours to make a decision.

Counter

First, you could question why this time limit is imposed. Second, you could use the principle of turning the screw. Tell the seller that this time limit is unacceptable. Third, you could change conditions. Tell the seller that you will have a partial answer within twenty-four hours with the full reply in x number of hours. This will give you more time to make a better decision. Fourth, you could ignore the limit set.

34. Principle of *Fait Accompli*

Fait accompli is a principle coined by Gerard I. Nierenberg. It has a lot in common with playing dumb. There are times when it is in your best interest to go ahead and do something without first negotiating it. Then, when you get caught, you simply respond along the lines of, "Who, me? I didn't know I wasn't supposed to be doing x. I apologize. We will not do that anymore."

Example

The first year we started our printing company we had saved about $20,000 to pay our sales tax. We knew exactly when it was due. But we also needed a new printing press. When loan officers at the bank said they would not extend our line of credit, we decided to use our money set aside for state sales tax to buy the new press. When the State Board of Equalization sent us a letter for the taxes, we said in shock, "We are so sorry, we did not know that the money would be due all at one time. This is our first year in business and we just did not know the rules."

The result was that we bought the press and worked out a great payment plan with the state board. It was even better than we could have done with the bank. Our company was happy, the state board was happy, and the bank was happy: a win/win/win outcome.

Counter

The reason this technique is so powerful is that there are few things you can do to counter it. What is done, is done. First, if you have the power to stop future progress, do so. With the process on hold, you are in a better position to force future concessions. Second, you can usually get some type of icing on the cake or other concessions.

35. Principle of Facts and Statistics

Any time you can add facts and statistics to your presentation, you have an added tool that your counterpart will find difficult to handle.

Example

Peter Ueberroth, the mastermind of the 1984 Los Angeles Olympics, used facts and statistics to his advantage when he negotiated the television rights to the games. Ueberroth studied the ratings and knew them inside and out. Several times the networks questioned him on his facts, and each time he proved he was right.

When you can use facts and statistics to your advantage, you add a tremendous amount of power and credibility to your case. But if you use them incorrectly, and your counterpart proves you wrong, you will lose your credibility. When this happens, you will have to fight twice as hard to gain any deal point.

Counter

First, question the validity of your counterpart's facts and statistics. Where did they come from? Are they applicable in this specific situation? Second, delay the negotiation process so that you can research and develop your own facts and statistics.

36. Principle of No Approval

The no-approval strategy involves taking an action without asking or negotiating it with your counterpart, then waiting to see what the counterpart's response will be.

Example

You are negotiating to lease space in an industrial building. The owner of the building sends you a lease agreement, and one of his conditions is that if you are more than ten days late on the rent, there will be a 5 percent late fee. Since you think the owner is desperate to lease the space, you cross out the 5 percent late fee, replace it with a 1 percent late fee, sign the lease, and send it back to the owner with a check. Now it is up to the owner to counter if he feels the 1 percent is unacceptable.

Counter

First, if the no-approval action is unacceptable to you, immediately counter back in writing. Second, you could refuse to negotiate further because the counterpart does things without your approval, which is unacceptable. Third, you could delay negotiations and see if you could generate other offers.

37. Principle of Taking a Different Angle

If you are a good communicator and are proficient at finding out your counterpart's needs, you can redefine an unacceptable offer and make it acceptable.

Example

You would like to hire a star salesperson for your company. Your boss has put a salary ceiling of $70,000 on salespeople employed at your company. Your problem is that the salesperson has a base salary of $75,000 at her current job and will not leave for less.

You decide to reopen the negotiations with a different proposal. You offer a base salary of $70,000 but you will give the salesperson a $15,000 bonus if she can reach sales of $500,000. This arrangement is more acceptable to your boss, and the salesperson sees no problem selling a half million dollars' worth of your product.

Counter

Use the principle of delay so you can evaluate their new proposal. Second, if you are still a distance apart, try splitting the difference.

38. Principle of Disassociation

At times, it may be to your advantage to associate your counterpart or the item you are negotiating for with someone or something unfavorable or undesirable.

Example

You are in the market to buy a house. You have looked at several houses in the neighborhood and like what you see. One house you looked at several blocks away had a cracked slab that was caused by poor soil drainage. When you find the house you like, you make an offer that is $15,000 below the owner's asking price. You tell the owner your offer is lower because it is common knowledge that the house was built on soil that has drainage problems. In fact, you even offer to show them the house that has the cracked slab.

Counter

First, you could delay decision making to see whether the information your counterpart has shared with you is correct. Also, the delay gives you an opportunity to plan your counter. Second, you could counter back at your original price or slightly lower. Third, you could use a trade-off concession if something else is very important to you. Fourth, you could flinch. Fifth, you could walk away.

39. Principle of Postponement

When a counterpart presents you with an offer, it is often in your best interest to delay your reaction or counteroffer until you have time to properly evaluate a counterstrategy.

Example

You want to build your own house. So you draw up plans with an architect and then send the plans to three contractors to get bids. When the proposals come back, you tell each contractor that it will take you two weeks to review the documents and get back in touch with them. The extra time gives you the opportunity to evaluate the contracts, prepare a strategy for each one, and verify any information that you do not think is correct or in your best interest.

Counter

First, if someone postpones your offer, when you finally get the counteroffer, buy time so that you can put together your best counterstrategy. Second, you could withdraw. Third, every time your counterpart delays, you can change what has been agreed to in the past. Use the principle of the withdrawn offer and raise the price. This lets your counterpart understand that delays will not be rewarded.

40. Principle of the Bluff

There will be times when it pays to bluff your counterpart. You say something with hope that your counterpart will not try to or cannot verify your information, hence call your bluff.

Example

The movie *Beverly Hills Cop* has a scene where a robber is holding Eddie Murphy hostage. One of the Beverly Hills detectives is holding a gun on the robber. The robber threatens that if the detective does not put down his gun, he will shoot Murphy. Murphy tells the detective that the robber is bluffing, that he doesn't have the guts to shoot him. Murphy orders the detective to shoot the robber. To everyone's surprise, including Murphy's, the detective shoots the robber right between the eyes. Murphy, furious that the detective had fired so close to his own head, said, "You S.O.B., I can't believe you did that! I was bluffing."

Counter

First, you can delay to get your ducks in a row. Second, you can provide your own facts and statistics to expose the bluff. Third, you can walk away.

41. Principle of Standard Practice or Policy

"Standard practice" is a tactic used to convince others to do or not do something because it does or doesn't fit standard policy. This strategy works well because it suggests that the way being proposed is the usual way to do whatever needs to be done and is probably a safe approach.

The most common example is the standard contract. The party being asked to sign a standard contract assumes it does not need to be changed. Most people will accept a "standard contract" as just that, standard. However, those who are willing to test just how "standard" the contract is usually have good results.

Example

A landlord hands you a lease to sign. As he shows you the lease, he states it is a standard California Apartment Association lease. He asks you to initial it in two places and sign at the bottom.

Counter

First, you could use the principle of the salami. Start slicing away, ever so slightly, at what is considered standard. Second, you could use the trade-off concession. Third, you could rewrite the contract. Fourth, you could take a part of the "standard contract" and tell your counterpart it is a non-negotiable demand. Fifth, you could walk away.

42. Principle of Never Saying Yes to the First Offer

Have you ever felt that you paid too much for something? Chances are you felt that way because you did not have to fight hard enough for your outcome. When someone says yes to your first offer, you walk away with one of two feelings. First, you think you paid too much. If that feeling is not enough to make you have buyer's remorse, you will probably think something is wrong with what you just bought.

Example

Buyer: "You are asking $15,000 for your car. Would you consider taking $14,000?"

Seller: "Sure, $14,000. It's a deal!"

Counter

First, this is the time to use the principle of the false alarm. Tell the seller you were only asking him if he would consider $14,000. That is still too much to pay. Now you had better raise your level of aspiration. Second, you could use the principle of higher authority. Tell the seller that $14,000 sounds reasonable, but you need your spouse to come over and take a look at the car.

43. Principle of Divide and Conquer

Sometimes the only way to penetrate your counterpart's band of solidarity is to try to divide his or her camp. This requires you to win over part of your counterpart's group. Slowly, you hope you can convince enough members of the group that your position is fair. Eventually, if you are successful, the portion of the group you persuaded will convince the rest of the group.

Example

In 1987, the National Football League Players' Association went on strike. The owners, not to be put out of business, formed all new teams. Before the first scab game, the players were united as any group could be. As the weeks progressed and the players realized the strike was not effective, they began to fight among themselves. Eventually, the players were going public with anger about their union president. By the third week, some of the players had even jumped ship and began playing with the scabs. On the side of the players' association, this strike was one negotiated blunder after another.

Counter

In the case of the players' association, the players should have asked for only the demands they could all agree on, then held fast. As it was, the union had to retract on what they had called an unretractable position, and in negotiation that is a no-no.

44. Principle of the Bandwagon

One of the most powerful closing techniques you can use in sales is to tell your buyer that everyone is buying your product. In fact, sales are going so fast that you can't keep the product on the shelf.

Example

Ten years ago, San Diego's investment community was struck by a Ponzi scheme run by an up-and-coming company called J. David. This investment company had the reputation of paying higher-than-average returns, and the word spread around the community like wildfire. Investors could not wait to jump on the bandwagon. As with all Ponzi schemes, many investors lost big when the scheme was exposed.

Counter

Walk away. In negotiations, if it sounds too good to be true, it probably is. At the very least, stand back and take a second look.

45. Principle of One Foot on the Dock, One Foot on the Boat

When a counterpart needs to negotiate with you, but he or she is making unreasonable demands or taking unreasonable delays, one option is to start withdrawing pieces of your original offer. Another alternative is to start adding punitive actions, creating the feeling that one foot is on the dock, the other is in the boat, and the boat is slowly moving away from the dock.

Example

The IRS is a great example of an organization that practices this tactic. If you have ever been late on paying your taxes, you know that with each letter the IRS sends, the penalties get worse. You do not have a choice. The negotiator needs to be involved, and the sooner the better.

Counter

With the IRS—prayer helps. It may also be helpful to use the services of an ex-IRS auditor. A second counter that may work with any other individual or organization is to use a tactic that effects the counterpart's ability to meet his or her needs and goals. If a bank recalls a commercial loan early and the corporation doesn't have the ability to repay the loan, the bank generally starts a slow constriction process. Raising interest rates, putting holds on deposits, restricting new credit, and uncomfortable meetings asking for personal guarantees are all in their negotiation strategy. One strategy that may have an effect on the bank's goals is for the corporation to threaten to declare bankruptcy.

46. Principle of the Ambush

Showing up to any negotiation in large numbers—and better yet, unexpectedly—has tremendous impact in a negotiation.

Example

A great example of the ambush occurred at a city council meeting where a developer was trying to get his project approved. Much to everyone's surprise, over 200 citizens showed up to oppose the project.

Counter

The best counter in this situation is advance preparation. If you are well prepared, you will know the magnitude of your opposition. A second effective counter is to request a postponement in the negotiation. The purpose of the postponement is (a) to regroup and reorganize strategy, and (b) to try a divide-and-conquer strategy with your counterpart.

Finally, you can sell the decision makers and counterparts on the benefits of deciding in your favor. In this particular example, the developer won his case by selling three things: the number of people his development would employ; the number of tax dollars generated for the city; and the willingness to work with a citizens' advisory group made up of some of the people opposing the project.

47. Principle of the Field Trip

Any time you can get your counterpart to leave his or her office and visit your site, or another customer's operation/installation, you will obtain leverage in the negotiation. The reason this approach works so beautifully is that your counterpart has to invest time and energy to come to your location. This time and energy usually help raise the counterpart's level of commitment. A second reason it works well is that your counterpart gets to see your operation functioning in real life. If your product or service is working well, most people will envision themselves using what you are offering in the negotiation.

Example

A salesperson who sells printing presses knows the value of getting a potential customer out to a customer's plant who is currently utilizing the model of press to be sold. Whether it be another customer's plant, the dealer's showroom, or a trade show, when the customer takes the time to see the press in action, two things happen. First, the customer invests his or her time. Second, if the demonstration works well, the customer sees happy customers utilizing the press. Many times, the customer can actually see him- or herself utilizing the press during the demonstration.

Counter

There are three effective counters when the principle of the field trip is utilized by your counterpart. First, once again, as long as you have the ability to walk away and not feel obligated to make a decision on the spot, you will maintain a balance in the negotiation. Second, you can create your own field trip...possibly to a plant where they are using a competitor's product. The more knowledge you gain for yourself about the competition and the product you are currently negotiating, the better off you will be. Third, you can actually seek out customers who are dissatisfied with the product in question. They will usually be a resource for information that will help you gain leverage with the salesperson.

48. Principle of the Presentation

A well-organized, well-researched, and well-presented negotiation is a powerful strategy that is available to everyone. The more effective your presentation skills, the better your ability to effectively communicate your needs.

Example

Former President Ronald Reagan and 1992 presidential candidate Ross Perot were both masters of using their presentation skills, combined with the media, to persuade the public. Besides strong verbal communication skills, both relied on visual aids to make their point.

Counter

There are three effective counters to this strategy. First, be equally or better prepared. Second, pick a master communicator to represent your side of the negotiation. Third, find errors in how your counterparts represent their information and bring the errors to their attention.

49. Principle of the Shark in the Moat

To be an effective negotiator, you need access to the person who has the knowledge and ability to negotiate. When you can't get past a secretary, you will find it difficult to negotiate. Some negotiators use this strategy to their advantage by either stalling the negotiation or using the shark in the moat as a good guy/bad guy technique.

Example

A commercial real estate professional was trying to secure an appointment with an executive of a major corporation. No matter how many times he called, he constantly reached the executive's secretary or voice mail. Each time the secretary's promise was the same, "I will give Shirley the message you called." Each time the secretary would call back with a small piece of information that would barely keep the negotiation going. The salesperson could slowly feel his leverage slipping and his frustration rising.

Counter

Call very early in the morning or very late in the afternoon when there is less chance that the shark will be on duty. Sharks tend to have set hours, and you need to work around them.

50. Principle of Feeling Hurt or Betrayed

Most negotiators, even the tough ones, want to avoid hurting someone else's feelings. The tough negotiators don't mind being ruthless and consider their actions just a part of business. What they don't deal well with are situations where someone tells them that they have hurt the person's feelings or betrayed him or her in some way.

Example

I was negotiating a subcontract for my services. In the middle of the negotiation, the contractor stopped and stated that it was important that I know how he felt. The contractor went on to tell me that he felt hurt and betrayed that I would not work for him unless I made a higher fee. He then cited our long business relationship as the context for his feeling hurt. I backed up and changed my aspirations because I felt bad that what I was doing was being taken so personally. I do not mind driving a hard bargain, but I do not want to hurt people's feelings in the process. Unfortunately, I learned the second time that this happened with the same person that it just might be a tactic.

Counter

Simply say, "I'm sorry." Ask them to clarify why they feel that way. It may also be helpful to ask them if they can understand, if they were in your shoes, why it would be important to obtain or achieve what you are asking for.

10

TEN STEPS TO SUCCESSFUL NEGOTIATION

Of all the things that we have the ability to practice and learn, negotiation is one of the most nebulous and complex. The following points, if practiced...and practiced...and practiced, will help you to become a better negotiator.

1. Recognize that everything in life is negotiable! From deciding who takes out the garbage in your house to determining what price you will pay for a product or service to merging your car into rush-hour traffic, everything is negotiable.

2. Go for win/win outcomes. Find out the needs and goals of your counterpart. Yes, you do have a vested interest in helping your counterpart meet his or her needs and goals, especially if you ever have to negotiate with that person again.

3. Aim high; the outcome will always be better with high aspirations.

4. Have sound strategies and tactics. If you know all the strategies and tactics outlined in Chapter 9, plus the counters to the strategies and tactics, you will always be able to maintain a balance in the negotiation.

5. Plan ahead and research well. If you wait until you enter into the negotiation to do your planning and research, you will be like a ship out at sea without a sail and a rudder. You will move with your counterpart but without strategic direction.

6. Listen more than you speak. To create a win/win negotiation, you will need to understand the needs and goals of your counterpart. It is impossible to do so without being a great listener.

7. When you do speak, ask great questions. The more you learn and understand about you counterpart's needs, the easier you will find it to create a win/win negotiation.

8. Learn to effectively read nonverbal communication. Remember only 7 percent of the total message comes from the spoken word.

9. Learn to identify your three negotiation counterparts, the sharks, carps, and dolphins. Remember that dolphins are the only negotiators who have the ability to strategically change their tactics when one does not work. Be like a dolphin.

10. In most negotiations you will have the ability to walk away. Remember, the side with the least commitment to the relationship usually holds the most power.

Go for it! Like any skill, with practice, you can be a great win/win negotiator.

APPENDIX

Endnotes

Chapter 1

1. Gerard I. Nierenberg, *The Complete Negotiator* (New York: Nierenberg and Zeif, 1986), p. 16.

2. Israel Unterman, class notes, Policy and Procedures Coursework, San Diego State University, 1983.

Chapter 2

3. *The San Diego Union,* May 12, 1992, p. A3. Niki Cervantes, "Ex-CIA Chief to Probe Response to Riots."

Chapter 6

4. Albert Mehrabian. *Nonverbal Communication* (Chicago: Aldine, 1972), p. 3.

5. D.A. Humphries. Researcher of study cited in G.I. Nierenberg and H. Calero, *How to Read a Person Like a Book* (New York: Cornerstone Library, 1971), p. 9.

Chapter 7

6. D. Lynch and P. Kordis. *The Strategy of the Dolphin* (New York: William Morrow and Company, 1988), p. 16.

Chapter 9

7. Lee Iacocca and William Novak. *Iacocca: An Autobiography* (New York: Bantam Books, 1984), p. 233.

Bibliography

Cohen, Herb. *You Can Negotiate Anything*. Secaucus, NJ: Lyle Stuart, 1980.

Donelson, Elaine. *Personality, A Scientific Approach*. Pacific Palisades, CA: Goodyear Publishing, 1973.

Gschwandtner, Gerhard. *Nonverbal Selling Power*. Englewood Cliffs, NJ: Prentice-Hall, 1985.

Karrass, Chester. *The Negotiating Game*. New York: Thomas Y. Crowell, 1970.

Kordis, Paul L., and Lynch, Dudley. *The Strategy of the Dolphin*. New York: William Morrow, 1988.

Nierenberg, Gerard I. *The Art of Negotiating*. New York: Simon & Schuster, 1968.

——. *The Complete Negotiator*. New York: Nierenberg and Zeif, 1986.

——. *Fundamentals of Negotiating*. New York: Hawthorn/Dutton, 1973.

——. *How to Read a Person Like a Book*. New York: Hawthorn/Dutton, 1971.

INDEX